BOB HAZEN, JANI IVERSON, AND ERIC VINES

Be a Better Board Member

*How to be the board member
you and your nonprofit deserve*

PAGE TWO
PARTNERS
LEADERSHIP SERVICES

First published by Page Two Partners 2020

Special thanks to our editor, Kyra Nourse, who went above and beyond.

First edition

ISBN: 9798691757501

This book was professionally typeset on Reedsy.
Find out more at reedsy.com

This book is dedicated to the nonprofit sector—to the board members, staff, clients, and foundations with whom we've shared success, failure, challenge, and change.

May that wisdom and experience inspire us all to continue building vibrant, healthy, equitable, and thriving communities.

Contents

INTRODUCTION

At the end of 2019 there were more than 1.7 million registered nonprofits in the United States. About two-thirds of these are 501(c)3 or public benefit charities, so named because they are supported by and are designed to benefit the public.[1] If you are reading this, you are probably a part of, or about to be a part of, at least one of these organizations. Roughly 25 percent of all Americans volunteer in some capacity with charity organizations and contribute billions of dollars each year to support them.

As a board member, your primary duty is to make sure that your nonprofit does in fact benefit the public. It is your responsibility to oversee the financial, legal, and moral well-being of the organization.

Nonprofit organizations play a large role in improving the lives of many, enhancing the health, safety, and cultural vitality of our communities. A 2019 report by the Center for Civil Society Studies at Johns Hopkins University states that nonprofits accounted for roughly one in 10 jobs in the U.S. private workforce, with total employees numbering 12.3 million in 2016[2]. Many more work in non-governmental organizations around the world. There are probably an equal or greater number of board members. People devote their time and energy because they want to make a difference, feel that they are doing something meaningful, and generally use their passion to benefit some part of their social world. By supporting the arts, health, sports, religion, and science, they engage their passions and create meaning. We believe that the better these organizations operate, the healthier our country and our society will be. The more effective that board members can be, the better things will operate.

The goal of this book is simple: to provide a training resource that quickly starts you on the path to learning what you need to know about

YOUR organization to be an effective board member. All organizations are different, and so what works for one might not work for all. We'll cover the basics—things that are true for almost all nonprofits; but we'll also help you ask the right questions, and we'll give you information that guides you toward becoming a helpful and confident board member.

As you go through the book, you will encounter lots of questions. These are designed so that you can determine whether you know what you ought to know about your organization. Each chapter also ends with review questions. If you can answer "yes" to all of these, you will have a good grasp of what you need to know about the topics covered in each chapter. If the answer is "no," you probably have a bit more work to do, more information to gather, or more conversations in which to to engage. If no one in the organization knows the answers, you should make a plan to get that information.

Being an effective board member starts before you join the board. Prospective board members can use this book as a tool to help choose a board that is a good fit for their skills and their passions. Joining a board that is not a good fit for you is not going to help the organization and will not be a meaningful experience for you. Before you accept an invitation to join a board, take the time to understand what will be expected of you. Look at what kind of board it is. Understand the culture, style, and competency of the organization and the board by attending a board meeting, participating as a volunteer, or having coffee with an existing member. Investigate how financially and programmatically stable the nonprofit is. This book will guide you to do that.

We believe it is important to place our work in social and historical context, so in chapter one, we begin with a brief history of the nonprofit sector in the United States.

Chapter two helps you find out what you should know before you join a board. Too often, people join a board with little understanding of what is expected of them. Someone who has never been a board member is unlikely to know how to be a good one. It takes more than common sense, though that helps. Often, when you join a board, you are trained (if there is any training) by people who don't have a lot more experience than you do, although they may know more about the programs and the culture and some of the details of the organization.

Chapter three gives you a concise, basic understanding of what to expect from your board orientation. Informed board members lead to a better functioning nonprofit, a more efficient use of resources, and, from our point of view, a better world.

Nonprofit organizations are structured so that board members, as part of the public, have overall authority over their respective organizations. They are responsible for their organization's financial, legal, and moral well-being. They ensure that these organizations are actually providing a public benefit in an ethical way. Chapter four takes you through your responsibilities.

Chapters five through seven address what makes a good board, the role of effective leadership, and some keys to having effective meetings. If you enjoy board meetings and they are productive, there's a good chance you're in a healthy organization.

There are a lot of details that you need to be aware of as a board member. Chapters eight through ten help you to understand your board's policies, to be able to clearly articulate the mission and values, and to gain clarity about the diversity and inclusion issues that are critical to the nonprofit sector and society at large.

Knowing the relationship between the board and the executive director, and having a good grasp of the financial, budgeting, and fundraising aspects of your nonprofit, are all essential to being an effective board member. We explore these areas in chapters eleven through fourteen.

As you spend more time on the board, you'll likely encounter issues such as strategic planning and board recruitment. Chapters fifteen and sixteen offer guidance on these facets of board service.

Finally, chapters seventeen through nineteen address evaluation, succession planning, and finding a new director. The average tenure for an executive director has traditionally been five to six years. As executive director work gets increasingly stressful, this length of time has been shrinking, so the odds are good that you will face this challenge sometime in your board experience.

Each chapter contains practical advice and success stories as well as cautionary tales. Each ends with a list of review questions to help you assess your process of learning.

There is no one-size-fits-all rulebook for boards. There are differences state to state. The law gives you flexibility in terms of how you operate your nonprofit, how many board members you have, how often you meet, what your relationship with the executive director is like, how much power and influence the chair has, and what kind of board you are.

Serving on a board brings deep satisfaction to many people. You might imagine this scenario: You are on the board of a food bank. Perhaps you were there when a young man walked into the office to say "your support helped me and my family survive for the past four months when I was out of work, but I just landed a job, and I wanted to stop by and thank you for changing my life."

Being on the board of a nonprofit can give you an opportunity to help address a social problem, expand the creative thinking of your community, provide food for the hungry, or offer health services to those in need. Since nonprofits have been leading the way in diversity, equity, and inclusion efforts, it can also be a great way to increase awareness of and be actively involved in important societal issues. Nonprofits provide a way to connect to your community, meet interesting people, feel good about your contributions, and be of true service to others. For those of us who have worked in this sector for years, it is a privilege and a responsibility we take seriously, and it can add meaning and delight to our lives. You are about to commit a lot of time, energy, and personal resources to your new nonprofit. It is worth learning how to do that as effectively as possible. The more you learn, the more enjoyable it will be, and the more usefully your time will be spent. We hope that you will find this book a helpful tool in making the most of your experience.

1. Candid (formerly Foundation Center and Guidestar) from the IRS Business Master File: https://www.issuelab.org/resources/36381/36381.pdf
2. Center for Civil Society Studies at Johns Hopkins University, 2019 http://ccss.jhu.edu/

1

A BRIEF HISTORY OF THE NONPROFIT SECTOR

Peole have practiced philanthropy in different ways since human beings first started to form social groups. Most people, if given the chance, choose to help make their society stronger, explore their creativity, and assist those in need. The ways we do that are almost limitless. It is through cooperation and generosity that communities survive and thrive.

Early institutional philanthropy in seventeenth century America was mostly about maintaining the power structure and the *status quo* by means of the creation of educational institutions or church groups. The first university, Harvard, was founded in 1636 to train clergy to serve the thousands of Puritans coming to New England. For the most part, states granted charters to institutions that promoted the prevailing agendas of the day and refused to grant charters to groups that confronted issues of slavery, segregation, or equal rights. More positively, on a community level, many fire departments and policing efforts were started as charitable organizations, rather than as state-run institutions.

After the great foment of the Civil War, the sector gradually expanded to include charity organizations such as hospitals, social service organizations, art museums, and performing arts groups. Many of the institutions that you are probably familiar with started in the latter half of the nineteenth century.

In 1867, the Peabody Education fund was created as perhaps the first modern independent foundation with a general purpose of supporting a broad number of causes, rather than a single institution. The Boys Club (later the Boys and Girls Club) was started in 1860 by three women to help address the challenges faced by young boys living on the streets. Howard University, the first Black University in America, was founded in 1867 as a training facility for black preachers. The first Settlement House in the US was started in 1886 in New York. In these houses, unrelated middle-class men and women lived together with immigrants and the poor to learn from them and to help them move out of poverty and fight discrimination. In 1887, the first United Way was formed in Denver, Colorado, to provide a single venue that solicited funds from the general public to support local charities and relief efforts. The Salvation Army grew in response to the disasters of the Galveston Hurricane of 1900 and the San Francisco earthquake of 1906. The NAACP was founded in 1909 by both white and black activists to begin to try to address some of the injustices of racism.

Wealthy individuals and social reformers continued to create a new landscape of charity and philanthropy in the late nineteenth and early twentieth centuries. John Andrew Carnegie, one of the first great philanthropists, wrote "The Gospel of Wealth" in 1899, asserting that all personal wealth beyond a family's necessity should be regarded as a trust fund to be used for the benefit of the community. His first job, after immigrating to the US from Scotland at age 13, was carrying bobbins to the workers for $1.20 a week. When he retired in 1901 after selling Carnegie Steel for $480 million (around $14 billion in today's dollars), he devoted himself to full-time philanthropy. We have our modern library system thanks to his generosity, with nearly 2,000 libraries financed by Carnegie.[1]

Other individual fortunes went toward private foundations controlled by one person or one family. Margaret Olivia Slocum Sage was a noted donor to educational institutions in the early 1900s. Julius Rosenwald, part owner of Sears, and John D. Rockefeller, once the richest man in America, gave away millions to educational causes as well.

The Revenue Act of 1913 changed the landscape dramatically with the institution of the federal income tax, while simultaneously exempting institutions promoting religious, charitable, scientific, or educational purposes from those taxes. It was two years later, in 1915, that the New York Times first recorded the use of the word "nonprofit." The Revenue Act of 1917 established an individual income tax deduction for contributions made to tax-exempt charitable organizations. This deduction was conceived as a way to encourage charitable contributions at a time when income tax rates were rising in order to pay for World War I.

The savings bonds program to support funding of World War II helped build the mindset of individual giving. Increased prosperity in the United States following that war prompted a significant rise in giving. The Revenue Act of 1954 established the tax codes as we know them today. Section 501(c) of the Internal Revenue Code stated that in order to enjoy tax-exempt status, a nonprofit institution must be organized and operated purely for nonprofit reasons, with none of its earnings going to any member of the organization.

By the 1950s, about 20,000 new nonprofit organizations were being started in the United States every year. In the 1980's, the Independent Sector, a nonprofit organization, was founded to bring together for the first time all elements of the national philanthropic community: nonprofits, foundations, and corporate giving programs. In the early 1990s, the pace of new startups had increased to about 50,000 annually. By 2019, there were approximately 1.7 million nonprofits in the US.

Nonprofits have gradually taken on a larger role in supporting the social fabric of our country. They are often on the front lines of addressing issues of racism and inequity in our society. In 2017, individuals, foundations, and corporations donated $410 billion to nonprofits. The breakdown of how those billions are roughly distributed is as follows:

31% to churches

14% to education

12% to human services

11% to foundations

9% to health

7% to public-society (voter and consumer rights)

    6% to international charities
    5% to arts and culture
    3% to the environment
    2% gifts to individuals[2]

These organizations vary in size from a few board members with no paid staff, to hundreds or even thousands of employees and assets of billions of dollars. One thing they all have in common, by law, is that they have a board of directors, usually with a minimum of three members and often many more. The board has ultimate responsibility for making sure laws are followed, money is well spent, and programs are aligned with the organization's mission.

Our society has become heavily dependent on the services of nonprofits. From healthcare to the arts, environmental protection to social services, the nonprofit sector blends a business structure with a public benefit. At the head of most of these nonprofits is a nonprofit leader (executive director or President/CEO), hired and overseen by a governing board made up of community members. This structure was put in place to ensure sound oversight of these organizations that receive tax forbearance in exchange for their good work. Despite being called "nonprofits," they need to make a profit (or at least break even) to stay in business; but unlike a regular business, any "excess" income must stay in the corporation. That profit can't be distributed to board members or anyone else; it must be used for the benefit of the organization and ultimately the community.

Nonprofits exist to make a difference in their communities, doing work that other businesses don't want to pursue or that the government is unable to do. In other words, the profit motive that drives most businesses is replaced with a service motive. Nonprofit governance was created to ensure that unscrupulous entrepreneurs don't try to game the system by setting up tax-avoiding enterprises that enrich the owners at the expense of community tax coffers. And in most cases, the system works pretty well.

That seems quite straightforward, but the reality is often far from simple. Human dynamics in the boardroom can be challenging in any organization.

While a for-profit business generally counts on alignment among board members around the desire to generate a profit, people join nonprofit boards for a wide range of reasons. Often, they want to help serve a social purpose. Sometimes, they want to be connected to a social group. And sometimes, they are just talked into it by a neighbor.

Best practices in board governance can mitigate the problems and enhance the efficacy of board members. Ultimately, the secret to creating a good board is similar to creating a good company. It's about first articulating and then standing behind your culture, values, and responsibilities. Attract the people you want to attract. Get to know people before you invite them to join the board. Have good systems and training for board members. Be clear about expectations and immediately work to address problems as they arise.

A great organization with a poorly functioning board will often become a poorly functioning organization. But a well-functioning board can solve problems and help restore smooth, effective operations to an organization with problems. It is your responsibility as board members to learn the rules, understand your obligations, and determine how to work together as a group. Board leadership matters.

1. The Carnegie Corporation, Andrew Carnegie's Story https://www.carnegie.org/interactives/foundersstory
2. The National Center for Charitable Statistics at the Urban Institute. Rounded to the nearest whole number: https://urbn.is/2SQwvT5 (Table 5)

2

WHAT YOU SHOULD KNOW BEFORE YOU JOIN A BOARD

L et's say a colleague from work or a next-door neighbor approaches you one day. "Hi, Joanne," he says. "I think you know I've been involved with a great organization that works with underserved kids. It's been such a meaningful experience for me, I thought I'd see if you might be interested in joining me on the board."

This chapter is designed to help both people in this hypothetical conversation. If you're being recruited, this will urge you to think about what you should know before you say yes. If you're already a board member, this information will help you prepare before you talk to someone. It's a big step to join a board, with legal responsibilities. The more you know about what awaits you, the better prepared you'll be to make a good decision.

When you serve on a board, you are essentially joining a family—a family that has a culture with rituals, practices, and rules that evolve over time. Your job is to learn those rules and practices so that you can work effectively in the group and bring value to the board and the organization.

The basics

As you consider joining a board, here are some basic questions to consider:

- What does the organization actually do? Does the mission spark your interest enough that you're willing to give up some other things in your life? If the answer is yes, or even maybe, then go ahead and find out more.
- Have you looked at the organization's website to see how they present themselves? Is the website up to date, with current information about staff, board, program, and publicity? How do they portray themselves on social media?
- Is it clear why you are being asked to be on the board, or what you are expected to do for the organization? Sometimes boards just need responsible people to fill the seats. Other times, they are looking for someone with financial resources to contribute, or someone with a network of people who who have the capacity to donate. Some groups seek candidates with experience and expertise in finance, marketing, governance, specific program skills, or capital campaigns. Make sure expectations are clearly articulated.
- What time commitment is required? If the group says, "We're just asking you to come to four board meetings a year and nothing more," understand that you won't be actively contributing very much. More likely, you'll soon be asked to do much more.
- What process does the organization use to bring you onto the board? Whom do you meet with? The executive director? The board chair? A committee?
- What information do they request from you? A resume or bio, an application, an interview, a statement of interest?
- Are you invited to attend a board meeting to see who is on the board and get a sense of the culture, style, and feeling of the meetings?
- Have you read the bylaws? They will tell you how the organization is structured and the length and number of board terms that you may be expected to serve.
- Is there an audit? It will give you financial information, but also reveal any issues that the auditor may have discovered.
- Is there a schedule for bringing on new board members?
- Is there a structured orientation and training for new board members?

- Is there a strategic plan? This will give you a good sense of what this nonprofit is expecting to accomplish in the next few years.

What kind of a board is it? There are a number of ways to label boards, but there are three main categories:

- **Governing boards** are engaged at a relatively high strategic level to help things run smoothly. They ensure that the executive director is leading properly and that the organization has sufficient resources, is focused on the mission, and has a clear strategic direction.
- **Fundraising boards** focus primarily on raising money to support the work of the organization, but they also, like governing boards, have overall responsibility for ensuring that the organization uses resources wisely and focuses on the mission.
- **Working boards**, in addition to governing and fundraising, do the mission work of the organization. Working board organizations might or might not have any paid staff to assist in carrying out the mission. As they grow larger and add staff, working boards might evolve into governing boards.

Of course, many boards do not fit neatly into these exact categories. If you are on a working board, you may well be expected to raise money and make high-level decisions about strategic direction. It's important to understand the main focus of your board. What type of board are you being asked to join?

What kind of an organization is it?

501(C)3 charities are the most common, and generally they allow supporters to deduct their donations from their taxes (if they itemize their deductions). There are three main types of public charities:

- Public charities are the best known. They have active programs and are primarily supported by donations.
- Private foundations, or non-operating foundations, do not have active

programs and are usually started, funded, and run by an individual, family, or small group.
- Private operating foundations have active programs.

Other tax exempt organizations:

- 501(C)4 charities are social welfare organizations, such as civic organizations or neighborhood associations. They may participate in politics as long as they spend no more than 50 percent of their money for that purpose.
- The others, from 501(C) 1 through 501(C)29, are focused on specific subjects.

Ask for the information you need

If you are not offered clarity about all the information listed above, you should ask for it! If your prospective board refuses or is unable to give you the information, you should probably consider serving a different nonprofit. Later in this book, we discuss the kinds of personal responsibility you'll accept by becoming a board member. Make sure you know what you are signing up for.

Once you have decided that you want to join the board, the current members will hold a vote before you are officially accepted as a member. For most organizations, the vote will take place at a board meeting, after members have had the opportunity to discuss your application.

Some nonprofits are what is called membership nonprofit corporations. A number of rules regulate membership organizations, but the most important is that new board members are elected by all of the members at an annual meeting, rather than by the board. The members may also have additional ability to oversee or restrict the decisions of the board. You should know if you are joining a membership nonprofit and what that means for you as a board member.

More in-depth questions

Now you've met the other board members, and you've seen how a board meeting operates and how it is facilitated. You've decided to embrace the mission of this organization and devote a substantial amount of time to helping it thrive. Let's move on to the next set of questions that you might want to ask to be sure that you really want to join. This is a lot of information, and the more you know, the more you will be aware of what you are signing up for, but don't let this scare you. It's a great opportunity to learn new skills!

Do you understand their financial situation?

We'll get into this more deeply in chapter 12, Loving your Financials, but you need to realize that, as a board member, you are responsible for the financial well-being of the organization. If you don't understand the organization's financial situation, how can you be responsible for it? Awareness of the financial details is essential.

You should examine four documents in particular. They might seem complicated if you're not familiar with them, but with a little help, you can unlock their secrets.

1 - The 990 is the tax return that nonprofits file each year

There are four different 990s: which one a given organization must file depends mostly on the size of the organization's budget. Larger organizations, with a gross income over $200,000, must use a regular 990. Between $50,000 and $200,000, a shorter form, the 990EZ, is used. Organizations with revenues under $50,000 per year file a very simple "postcard" 990. The fourth type, 990PF, is for private foundations.

If the accounting uses a calendar year, meaning the financial year ends on December 31st, the 990 is due by May 15th. If there is a different financial year end, for example June 30th, the 990 is due four and a half months later—though it is easy to get an extension.

You can access 990s for almost any nonprofit in the US by going to Guidestar (www.guidestar.com); it collects profiles and information on every registered nonprofit. You must be a member to get the 990s, but you can sign up and join for free.

The 990 contains a lot of information, but let's concentrate on the basics on the first page. This section will be easier to understand if you have the 990 in front of you so get a copy from the nonprofit you hope to join, or go online and get it from Guidestar.

The 990 will have the following categories:

REVENUE
Contributions and grants
Program service fees
Investment income
Other revenue
TOTAL revenue

EXPENSES
Grants paid
Benefits paid to members
Salaries, other compensation, benefits
Fundraising expenses
Other expenses
TOTAL expenses

What to look for on the 990

- Is revenue more or less than expenses? Revenue might be less than expenses in any given year for a lot of reasons. It is not necessarily a problem, but you should understand why. In general, your organization should be trying to add to its assets each year to provide a cushion for new projects or hard times.

- Is the income from different places, or is it all from one source? Ideally, a balance will exist between program fees, grants, and contributions, so that if one area falls short, it doesn't cripple your nonprofit.
- Compare this year's 990 to previous years to see the trends.

2 – The latest profit and loss (P&L) statement

The profit and loss statement, also called the statement of activities, is a monthly or quarterly statement that has many of the same categories as the 990, but it will include more detail and provide a more recent financial view. Generally, you can expect the P&L for a given month to be ready by the end of the following month; i.e., the P&L for May should generally be available by late June or early July.

What to look for on the P & L statement

- To understand the financial strength of the nonprofit, look at the P&L statement as you did the 990. The P&L will have much more in-depth information than the 990 about specific expenses and income. Compare how expenses and revenues are trending compared to the previous year.
- Are the financial documents up to date? If not, it is important to understand why. Whether someone is trying to hide something, or is simply unable to provide current financial information, consistently late financial statements are often a sign of a problem that must be addressed.

3 – The balance sheet

The balance sheet, also called the statement of financial position, shows how much money and assets the nonprofit has and how much is owed (liabilities).

What to look for in Assets:

- How much money is held in savings and other accounts? In organizations with a regular cash flow throughout the year, three to six months' worth of expenses is a healthy amount to have available.

- Are the assets going up or down? You can see this by comparing the current balance sheet to past years' balance sheets.
- What is the value of the physical assets, such as buildings and property owned by the organization?
- How much of that value has been "used up" (depreciated)? If you own a building that is almost fully depreciated, has the money been set aside so that it is available for repairs or replacement? For example, if a vehicle is fully depreciated, has money been saved to buy a new one?

What to look for in Liabilities:

- How restricted are the assets? Is the money tied up with donor restrictions that are indicated in the liabilities section? This is a tricky difference from for-profit accounting that board members often miss, and it can dramatically affect the ongoing viability of an organization.
- Are there any loans outstanding?
- Are there other debts?

One organization with which we worked told their incoming executive director that the organization had a year's worth of revenue in reserve to provide a runway for revamping and restructuring the organization. One month into her tenure, the executive director discovered that most of the reserves were "restricted" for pass through projects and that, in reality, the organization had only one month of actual reserves. She had to lay off her entire staff and cut programs. The board members, many of whom worked in the finance industry, did not distinguish restricted from unrestricted funds and hadn't bothered to investigate the difference.

4 - The annual budget

The annual budget shows what the organization expects its income and expenses to be for the year. The budget is a roadmap of the emphasis and expectations of a given year.

What to look for in the budget:

- First of all, is there an approved annual budget? The board should generally approve the projected annual budget by the start of the year and revisit it in depth at the six-month mark to decide on any necessary changes.
- Does the budget project a net profit, even a small one, so that you can increase the organization's reserves?
- If the budget projects a loss, this could be a worrisome sign. You should understand why this is proposed. Is it just for this year, or has there been a deficit for several years? How will it be replenished?
- Do the totals for revenue and expense look similar to previous years' actual revenues and expenses? What is changing from year to year?
- If income is projected to increase substantially, is this realistic, or just a reflection of someone's hopes and dreams?

There's a good chance that you don't have a lot of experience reading these kinds of documents. Most people don't. Don't hesitate to meet with the board treasurer, the executive director, or the financial officer, if there is one, to understand the budget. If any of these people don't seem to understand the financial statements, that is a red flag.

What are the board meetings like?

- What is the texture of the meetings? Are they long and tedious? Fast moving? Free-wheeling? Organized? Is there a strict agenda, or are things more relaxed? Do members laugh and have fun? Is it combative or uncomfortable? Do people come prepared? Was anything accomplished, or did people just read reports?
- The odds are good that whatever meeting you just sat through is going to

be a lot like the rest of the board meetings you'll attend for the next few years. If you enjoyed it, you're on the right track. If it was painful, you should determine whether what you experienced was an aberration, or a normal meeting.

What is it about the way the organization carries out its mission that excites you?

- You are excited, aren't you? If you are joining a board just to bolster your resume, please don't. You need to care about the organization, because it will take your time, money, and energy to participate, and you should feel a passion for the mission.
- Do you have time to contribute in the areas where the board expects a contribution? Are your skills going to be useful in the context of this organization?

How much money does the organization expect you to give or raise?

- This can be a hard subject to bring up, but clarity up front will save you from awkward questions later. Nearly every nonprofit expects some level of contribution. It could be $50, or it could be $50,000. Some have minimum levels of donation. If you cannot personally donate at the expected level, can you raise that amount from your friends or colleagues?
- Perhaps you are about to retire, and you're not sure how much money you will have available. Is there flexibility in how much you can give?
- One suggested rule of thumb is that if you are on a board, your donation to that organization should be in the top three of your yearly charitable contributions. It should be an amount that is significant for you.

What do you personally want to get out of serving on the board?

- Perhaps you also want to connect with other board members. Maybe you want to better understand homeless issues by working with a community shelter. Do you want to learn more about developing your leadership, fundraising, or financial skills?

- Whatever your motivation, be honest about your interests and be prepared to commit your heart to the organization's success as well as your own. A personal goal is often a good motivator for joining a board as long as you also believe in their work.

Is the board realistic about its own organization?

- Do the members of the board have a solid sense of the strengths and weaknesses that will affect their ability to move forward? Are they open about challenges, such as difficult board member personalities, thin finances, or a declining donor base?

How much time does board service require?

- There will be monthly, quarterly, or (at least) annual meetings. Will there be additional committee work? Will there be programs to attend, fundraisers and galas to support, and check-in meetings with other board members or the executive director? Being on a board takes time.
- If you don't have the time to give, you might want to look at other ways to support the organization instead of actually being on the board.

How far in advance are meetings set, and how many can you miss each year?

- If the board has two meetings per year and you miss one of them, is that acceptable? How flexible is your schedule to attend board meetings? Perhaps you take month-long camping trips every year, or have another personal commitment every month that might interfere with attendance. Perhaps you are a frequent traveler. Can you attend meetings remotely by phone or teleconference?

What does the organization do to prepare you to make a decision about being on the board?

- Do they provide the kinds of information we have suggested, or do they wait for you to ask? Are they surprised that you asked?
- Do you meet with the executive director? The board chair? Other board members?
- Do they ask about your skills and interests and why you want to join this board?

Additional documents and information

Below is a list of other information that will help you understand the organization you are about to join. You shouldn't hesitate to ask for these materials. Not all of these may be available, but many should be.

- **Cash flow projection:** This helpful document shows how much money is expected to come in and go out each month for the year. The budget may show adequate annual income to cover expenses, but if most of that money doesn't come in until the end of the year, you may have a cash flow problem. It's important to know how the flow of cash looks.
- **Line of credit:** It is important to know whether your organization has an available line of credit, how much, if anything, has been borrowed against it, and what the expected repayment plan is.
- **A list of primary programs**
- **A strategic plan**
- **A copy of the audit or financial review by an accounting firm**
- **An annual report**
- **The bylaws:** These should outline the rules of board membership and list the positions and terms of any officers.

This is a lot of information, but remember that, as a board member, you have responsibility for the financial health, and potentially the debts, of the organization you are joining. You don't want to join a board only to discover that the organization is about to run out of money. You also don't want to join a board that doesn't know if it is running out of money. Asking for these documents will help you be aware of the true situation.

If you don't understand how to read any of those documents, don't be shy about admitting it and getting help. The willingness and ability of people to explain these documents to you will tell you a lot about the attitudes and the level of understanding of the other board members and the executive director.

Options in lieu of being on a board

You might strongly support the mission of a nonprofit and want to help them. But after initial exploration, you may decide that you don't want the responsibility or the time commitment of being on the board. Perhaps it's just not the right time for you. There are alternative ways to offer support.

Are you well connected in the community and able to make introductions to politicians or wealthy people? You might offer five hours a year to help connect board members to important people. It might be an hour here and there, or it might be all at once. This kind of offer forces the organization to be really clear about how they want to use your expertise, avoids wasting time, and often results in both parties feeling like they've used the time wisely.

> One organization whose board I served on was seeking new members.
> Someone mentioned a well-known local philanthropist who was on
> several other boards, but who had shown interest in our mission. I
> suggested we brainstorm exactly how we might best use her skill sets
> and connections. In the end, we suggested an introduction to a friend of
> hers that we had been trying to approach. That friend became a large
> donor. We got two hours of time from our philanthropist, and it was
> enormously beneficial to us. We also learned that we could go back to
> her in the future if necessary.

What are other ways to be helpful? You might help by participating in a fundraising meeting, answering a question about insurance, or providing information about board structure or finance. You could offer to assist with an annual event, help the organization find a web developer, or get your law firm to provide pro-bono services. Don't hesitate to think of ways other than board service that a supporter might contribute.

People often underutilize the first six to nine months of their board service. They spend that time trying to understand the organization when they might have been working on programs or fundraising. If you explore and ask the right questions in advance and then decide to join, you can contribute from the beginning.

REVIEW QUESTIONS:

- Do you have a good picture of what the organization does?
- Do you understand the financial stability of the organization?
- Do you clearly understand what is being asked of you as a board member?
- Do you know whom to ask when you have questions?
- Are you energized by the thought of being closely involved with this organization for the next several years?

3

BOARD ORIENTATION

Y ou already know a fair amount about your prospective organization thanks to all the questions that you asked while you were trying to decide if this board is a good fit for you at this particular time. Now let's talk about the basic elements that you'll need to understand as soon as you join the board. Some organizations assign a "buddy" to new board members for the first six months. This gives you someone specific to talk with about your new role: your buddy will help you feel comfortable and find answers to your questions—including the questions posed in this book. Other organizations set up meetings between the new board member and the executive director, the board chair, or other board members or senior staff.

What should be covered in your orientation?

Get the right tools to be effective.

- What equipment do you need? If some or all of the board meetings are by ZOOM, Skype, or phone, do you have a good computer, iPad, or phone to participate fully in this role? Have you downloaded the software and practiced using it? If you or other board members don't have the necessary equipment, is there a plan to provide it? If you aren't comfortable with technology, will the organization provide the training you require to participate effectively? If the organization presents financials using Excel, do you have the software to view them, and more importantly, has the organization made sure that you are comfortable doing so? Can you access and read the minutes? Not everyone has the latest technology. That's okay. Every orientation should include IT training so that members can practice and master the tools they will need. We've seen many examples of people who thought they knew how to use a tool, discovered they didn't, and were then too embarrassed or frustrated to ask for help.

Understand the finances of the organization.

- As a board member, you are responsible for ensuring that the finances of your organization are well looked after. You have to understand them to be able to do that. During your initial assessment of the organization, you will have learned enough about the finances to be pretty sure there aren't any big surprises right around the corner. Now it's time to learn how to keep an eye on things and make sure that, going forward, money matters stay under control. Remember, it's not just the treasurer or the financial officer or the executive director who is responsible for the finances. Every board member bears fiscal responsibility. If you see a nonprofit with financial problems, chances are good that the board members haven't been paying close enough attention.

Learn the programs.

- The programs are the reason your nonprofit exists. Knowledge of these programs and their results is an important facet of being an effective board member. One of the best ways to learn is to volunteer and experience how your programs are run. Is it a food pantry? Go and spend some time handing out food, see how the staff run the program, meet some of the clients. Is it an animal shelter? Go help out at the shelter. Just remember, when you volunteer, you report to the staff member in charge. Take off your board hat, and remember you're a volunteer, not a boss.

You can ask several kinds of questions to better understand your programs:

- Who is helped by the program?
- What results does the program produce?
- How is success of the program measured?
- Are the programs having their intended effect?
- How is the program funded?
- What are some stories that you can share to show the effect of the programs on the community?
- Who else in the community has similar programs, and what can you learn from them?

Although nonprofits are structured so that the executive director reports to the board, and issues involving the staff almost always go through the executive director, this doesn't mean that you shouldn't meet some members of the staff. One common issue is that the board is often very remote from the staff. The staff members feel that board members don't understand how the programs work, who the members of staff are, and how they accomplish their goals. Make arrangements through the executive director to meet some of the staff so that you can see what is happening on the ground. Some organizations have photos and bios of both staff and board members on their websites. Spend some time making sure that you recognize people and can acknowledge their work.

Understand staff and board responsibilities.

- Especially if you are new to the nonprofit world, it is important that you understand what you, as a board member, are responsible for, and what the staff is responsible for. This is a theme throughout the book. By getting a basic overview from the board chair or executive director, you can avoid many boundary issues during your tenure.

Know the mission statement and your elevator speech.

- Learn to say quickly and compellingly what your organization does. Learn the mission statement. If it's too long to memorize easily, try putting it into your own words and explaining why the impact is important to you. If it sparks someone's interest, and you're asked questions, you can talk more about what your organization actually does.

- Craft a 15–30 second "elevator speech," a quick statement that expresses the need for the organization's programs, how that need is met, and why you personally are excited about it. Some boards start their meetings with a board member practicing an elevator speech or sharing a mission moment—this tends to energize people and gives others good ideas about how they might talk about the organization. Typical elevator speeches might go something like these three examples:

Children in our community are drinking water containing high levels of lead or other pollutants. We help find the resources needed to set up clean drinking water supplies and improve the health of our children. I know, because my children go to an affected school. We've already provided clean water to 20 schools in our community, but there are 30 more that need help.

There are very few arts programs in our elementary schools. Research has shown that having music and arts programming increases attendance and improves grades. We raise funds to supplement the arts programs in public schools. My daughter has started to look forward to going to school again now that she has taken up the clarinet.

We are creating sustainable models of food distribution for low-income communities. 30 percent of low-income children in our community don't have enough to eat until they get to school. We've given out 20 percent more food this year than last year, but we're still only reaching 50 percent of the families in need.

Use language that feels comfortable to you—something that personalizes the mission and conveys why you are personally involved. Talk to friends who are on other boards and see how they talk about their organizations. Do they move and inspire you? Learn from them.

- Be aware of the details and calendar for the year.
- Make sure that you have scheduled the board meeting dates and any important events.
- Get involved with something specific.
- Find a project that interests you: this is a great way to immerse yourself when you first join the board.

> *One arts organization had a deadline for a small, but quite promising, operational grant two days after my first board meeting. The executive director wasn't tracking application deadlines closely and wasn't experienced in writing grants. He was worried that he wouldn't be able to get this grant finished in time so I offered to help. It was challenging to pull this together in such a short time frame, but we got the grant finished (it was awarded), and when it was done, I had developed a good relationship with the director and knew as much as most of the other board members about the organization.*

REVIEW QUESTIONS

- Do you understand clearly the programs of your nonprofit and what problems they seek to address? Can you communicate that to friends?
- Have you developed a personalized elevator speech about your nonprofit?
- Do you understand the basic financial picture, the annual budget, the main sources of income, and the financial health of the organization?
- Is the annual meeting calendar set? If not, can you ask for it?
- Have you found a specific project that you can take on that makes you feel a part of this board and that feels satisfying to you?

4

BOARD MEMBER RESPONSIBILITIES

C hapters two and three covered the information you need to help make a decision about joining a board, and what should be included in a basic orientation. Now that you've decided to join and have the basics under control, make sure that you clearly understand your responsibilities.

Board members have a legal, financial, and moral responsibility for their organization. They are expected to put the good of the organization above anything else, including any personal reward for themselves or their friends. This means that they are responsible for how an organization treats people. For example, it is important to have good policies addressing harassment; but more importantly, everyone must be trained to understand what harassment means and how to avoid it. If you are trying to diversify your organization and make it more inclusive, board members and staff must be given the support that they need to achieve this objective.

"I didn't know" is not an acceptable excuse for doing something wrong. While the legal structure of the board protects you against casual mistakes, it doesn't protect you in cases of gross negligence or fraud. Even if you may not be financially liable for mistakes that your organization makes, you should carefully oversee how it operates. You shouldn't join a board unless you have the time, energy, and dedication to pay attention and help guide the board and the organization as well as you can.

Board members must make sure that they understand what the organization does, are aware of how it spends its money, and know how well it treats its employees. Board members need to ask questions until they know what is happening; and the organization is obliged to provide this information to the board members.

Frequently, new board members will be given a "board book" that has some or all of the following information in it. If your organization doesn't normally do this, ask for the information. You should take the time to read and understand the details and get any help that you need.

A typical board book would include the following information:

- A list of board members and contact information, along with a schedule of board terms, so that you know when people will be either renewing their board service, or leaving the board.
- Bios or resumes of board members, so that you can see what other skills and interests they have and what other organizations they support.
- A list of all board officers, their terms of office, and job descriptions for their positions. Typical positions include board chair, vice chair, secretary, and treasurer. The secretary is responsible for writing and submitting minutes, unless there is a staff person assigned to take minutes, while the treasurer bears overall responsibility for the financial oversight of the organization. The treasurer is also tasked with making sure board members are kept informed of the financial status. We'll present more information about the board chair position in chapter seven.
- A calendar of all board meetings and committee meetings for the year, as well as any important events, such as big fundraisers, annual parties, or major program events.
- The board meeting minutes for the past year. These will tell you if they are organized, readable, and up-to-date, as well as what issues have been discussed and what decisions have been made.
- The bylaws and the articles of incorporation. These will tell you the length of board-member terms, how many terms members usually serve, and if there are term limits. The articles of incorporation will show you that the

IRS has granted nonprofit status and clarify what type of status.

- An organizational chart showing names and positions of all the staff and who reports to whom.

- The conflict of interest agreement, which you must sign annually, and, if available, a copy of the whistleblower and harassment policies. These are discussed more fully in chapter ten.

- The timing and process for board evaluation of the executive director. If there is no process in place, and/or if it has been more than a year since a review happened, you should understand why and work toward conducting a review.

- Leases and contracts. Look at all major contracts, keeping in mind that grants are contracts: the organization has made a commitment to perform certain activities in exchange for the grant money it receives. If there is a lease for your organization's office or other property, you probably don't need to read it, but you should know when it is going to expire, and if there is a large rent increase looming. You don't need to read all the grants, but it is good to be familiar with the larger grants, what they promise to do, if there are any restrictions on their use, and when they expire.

- A list of the bank accounts (although not the bank account numbers) and banking relationships, including any line of credit that is available, the amount and how much has been withdrawn against it, and who has authority to draw on it. You should also know who all the signers are on the accounts.

- If there is an endowment or a large reserve, you should look at the investment policy that governs it, understand who is looking after it, and be clear about the policies governing withdrawals. Even if you don't understand all the details, it is important to be certain that there are guidelines in place that the leaders in the organization understand and follow.

- Property and liability insurance policies. It is generally the executive director's responsibility to ensure that the coverage is appropriate, but you want to know that insurance is in place and that there is an annual review to update coverage.

- Directors and officers (D&O) insurance. This is an important one. Most organizations have this type of insurance, and it would be rare not to need it. If yours is a small to medium-size organization, it might cost from one to a few thousand dollars a year. The predominant need for this stems from the risk of lawsuits. Typically, these are brought by an unhappy employee who has been let go, or been harassed, or faced other types of discrimination. Your insurance agent can explain the broad variety of possible scenarios that you should be aware of. While your status as a board member may well protect you from personally having to pay damages, legal bills can grow very rapidly when an organization tries to defend against this type of situation. D&O insurance is designed to cover legal costs as well as any damages that are awarded. Thus, both you and the organization are covered from most damages. Without insurance, this could be a fatal financial blow to your nonprofit. Many organizations invite their insurance agent to come to a board meeting every year or two to review the coverage and address changes in the laws that affect that coverage.

I was invited to a board meeting by the president of a small nonprofit who wanted me to join the board. When I asked if they had directors and officers insurance, there was an awkward look around the table and a pause. The board chair responded that they just used their homeowner's insurance. They hadn't realized that homeowners insurance is not designed for, and rarely covers, the kinds of situations D&O insurance does.

There are also some financial situations that no insurance will cover, and thus it is extremely important that you make sure they do not occur. Here are some possible scenarios:

- Perhaps your executive director has elected not to pay the IRS for payroll taxes, because the budget was just too tight. "We'll pay those when we get some more money in," she thinks to herself. But that day might never arrive. This is a situation that should never occur, and, with proper oversight, it never will. The IRS can come directly after board members to get their money back.

- If a board member personally guarantees a line of credit for the organization, that person may forget having done this, but the bank won't. We've run into situations where board members signed on to an account when the organization was first started, but they never signed off. Ten or twenty years later, if the loan is unpaid when the organization decides to close down, the loan liability still follows the long-departed board member who forgot to get her name off of the loan. No matter how much you love your organization, you should be very reluctant to personally guarantee a loan or line of credit unless you are willing to consider it a donation.

As noted previously, in cases of gross negligence or fraud, board members can be held accountable. If there is something that you, as a board member, should have known but didn't bother to look into, you could be on the hook for it.

Fortunately, these situations are somewhat rare and shouldn't deter you from board service. They should, however, serve as a cautionary tale. Understand what you are signing up for, and make sure that you are paying attention and that the organization's directors and officers insurance policy is up to date.

Documenting what you decide

Many organizations have an agreement that is reviewed every year that spells out what the board members commit to do and to give that year. Sometimes, this agreement is called a "board contract" or "board member agreement." It needn't be overly detailed, but it should clarify expectations as to board members' responsibilities, providing an additional opportunity for conversations about any issues that are unclear. This can be a great way to articulate how you intend to support the organization, as well as an opportunity to identify what you will need to be successful as a board member.

The board's role in communications

Who speaks for the organization, what do they say, and when do they say it? This can be an important point when something difficult happens.

> *One of those big summer storms flooded a pet shelter. Most of the animals were saved, but a couple of dogs didn't make it. A customer came in, saw what had happened, and alerted the local paper. The reporter assigned to the story got the name of a board member from a person on staff and called him up. He got one story. The reporter then called up the executive director who told him a different story. Even though the shelter had handled the emergency well, it looked in the press as though they were trying to cover up something, and it resulted in a lot of bad publicity.*

It is important to know who is designated as the spokesperson in any emergency. Everyone should be aware of who that person is so that any calls can be referred to the right person.

Even when there is no crisis, it is important for the organization to "stay on message." If your organization has a new program, and various people in the organization are describing it differently, the result can be confusing. Uncoordinated messaging is a growing problem as more people use social media, such as Facebook and Instagram, to share their lives and the things about which they feel strongly. Be clear about what kinds of things (relating to the organization) can and should be shared on social media and what should not.

In general it is the staff's role to implement the communication policies, but the board should have an oversight role to make sure that things are being done well. This is especially important in smaller nonprofits that don't have a full-time communications person or IT department. Here are some questions to consider in relation to communications, social media, and security:

- Are there sensitive topics that you should be aware of when representing the organization? Are there groups that oppose your mission that you should know about?

- What guidelines and rules govern the organization's use of social media? Who is overseeing your organization's different platforms? What can and should board members say about the organization and its programs on their own social media platforms?
- How do you stay up to date with the activities of the organization (website, press releases, LinkedIn, Twitter, Instagram, Facebook, TikTok)?
- Does the organization provide talking points for any issues in which the organization is engaged?
- Is the website being hosted securely? Is the member and donor information secure?
- When employees leave, what kind of systems do you have in place to control access to sensitive information? When the organization sets up social media accounts, are they set up in the name of the organization, rather than as a personal account of an employee? If set up as a personal account, the employee who created it could leave, but continue to post information that will then look like it is coming from the organization; or the employee could depart with a thousand followers (who thought they were following the organization).
- Are your organization's website and other social media sites checked frequently to make sure that everything is up to date? It is quite common to see notices about events that took place a year ago still being advertised. This reduces your credibility. As a new board member, bring fresh eyes to review how your nonprofit appears on social media.

The staff's understanding of the board's role

One issue that arises is that members of staff often have limited understanding of the function of the board. Staff orientations should include information about the role and authority of the board. Members of staff should understand that board members are volunteers who give their time and money to support the work of the nonprofit.

In addition, it's important for staff to realize that board members have access to information that requires confidentiality. As a board member, be careful about sharing information with staff members who might put that confidentiality in jeopardy. This withholding of information from the staff might make you as a board member seem distant or elite, but it's the executive director's job to share information with the staff, not yours. If members of staff aren't getting important information, then it's the board's job to manage the executive director and her execution of her role.

Members of staff should be given the option to come to the board if they have concerns about the organization or about the executive director's leadership that cannot be handled by talking with their supervisor, but there should be a clear process established for handling this kind of communication.

The board needs to understand and respect that the staff is implementing the programs, the reason for the nonprofit to exist. They often know the community better, have a clearer understanding of the capacity of the organization to do the work, and live the mission every day. As a board member, your job is to support them in this work.

REVIEW QUESTIONS

- Do you clearly understand what responsibilities and duties you are taking on by being on this board?
- Are your commitments written down and discussed with another board member or the chair so that everyone clearly understands what you have agreed to?
- Do you know which areas are your responsibility as a board member, and which areas are the responsibility of the staff?
- Do you know what to do and with whom to talk if you are unclear about any of these questions?
- Do you know how to access information using the tools that the organization has made available to you?
- Do members of staff recognize board members by sight? Do board members recognize at least some members of staff by sight?

5

WHAT MAKES A GOOD BOARD

Have you ever been to a board meeting where people were genuinely enjoying each other's company? Perhaps a few technical questions were raised, and someone knew the answer or where to get it. Maybe there were several small projects that needed doing, and someone immediately volunteered to do them. The board might have addressed a substantive issue, with information provided in advance, and then had a discussion that helped you see things in a new way, followed by a group decision to move forward. If you've had any of these experiences, you know how exciting it is when things come together and you have a board with the right chemistry, respect, talent, and size.

Chemistry and respect

Just as you don't always become friends with your coworkers, you can't expect to be best friends with everyone on your board. Perhaps you've been on a board or participated in meetings with people who disagree with everything that is said, who talk just to hear the sound of their own voices, or who are never prepared, but still insist on sharing their opinions. If so, you know the importance of style, chemistry, and respect. You need to get to know people before you ask them to join the board. Even one difficult person can turn a pleasurable two-hour meeting into what feels like a miserable ritual of group torture. We'll talk about this more in the section on board recruitment.

Talent

Having board members with the skills that your board needs, or the ability to connect to those skills, is essential. A common strategy is to develop a matrix that lists on one side the various skills that the board is seeking, and on another axis, the names and skills of the board members. Compare these to see which skills are covered by the current board membership, and which are lacking. Many boards look for the following skill sets to round out board membership:

- **Nonprofit financial expertise.** Nonprofit finances are not the same as for-profit finances. Having someone on the board who can understand your organization's financial picture is a crucial part of board oversight. Most successful boards have this person acting as treasurer, but don't assume that all financial advisors or even CPAs will understand nonprofit accounting—or will want to volunteer doing the type of work they do professionally.
- **Legal expertise.** Bringing a lawyer on to the board can be helpful to give guidance, though they may not specialize in areas that you need. A contracts attorney probably won't be an expert on employment issues or bylaws. Often, having a lawyer on the board can give your organization access to that person's law firm, or to a colleague at another firm. These might provide pro bono service and cover a wide range of topics.
- **Program expertise.** Whether your nonprofit organization is a food bank, an environmental group, or an arts organization, you want people with a passion for your mission. It can also be helpful to have board members with backgrounds and training in your program areas. Be aware that the organization has staff to run the programs, and well-meaning board members can sometimes get in the way more than they help. Be clear upfront about how a board member's expertise might be used and who has the authority to make decisions.

- **Fundraising.** If you do substantial fundraising, you probably have a fund development committee. A board member with experience in raising money and willingness to lead that committee can help the rest of the board get excited about fundraising efforts. Because this is such an important part of board duties, we'll expand on this in chapter 16.
- **Governance and personnel issues**. A board member with professional HR experience can be an enormous help. Staying on top of changes in the law related to employment issues and governance can be facilitated by someone with expertise in these areas. Be aware that board members should not be involved in specific staff personnel issues.
- **Community connections.** A board member with ties to the community can introduce you to the people who have the ability and capacity to get things done. Maintaining connections with past board members can also facilitate these essential introductions.
- **Marketing and communication**. Most smaller nonprofits need help in this area, because these tasks are often handled by whomever is available rather than a person with expertise. A board member with these skills can provide advice on a marketing and communications plan. Don't expect the board member to actually do all of the marketing and communications!
- **Information technology.** IT skills can be expensive to hire. Many nonprofits suffer from an out-of-date website, an obsolete backup system, or a network system that barely functions. An expert in this area is a boon to an organization, especially in smaller nonprofits without a tech person on staff or contract. With increasing reliance on electronic communication, it's important to have people who can guide you through security issues, or how best to use video conferencing services.

Volunteers

Keep in mind that you don't necessarily need someone to be a board member to get that person's help in these areas. When you join a board, you take on responsibilities and potential liabilities. Some people may believe strongly in your mission, but not want to attend board meetings or take on liability.

They may be willing to donate a few hours when specific problems arise in their areas of expertise. Keep a list of friends and what they can provide if you call them.

Size

Some boards have three members and some have 70. What is the right size for your organization? Larger boards can be unwieldy and inefficient, whereas really small boards may not have the person-power to get everything done. Small boards can be almost shut down by the sudden loss of one or two members. Boards smaller than five or six can be nimble, but they may lack the robust set of skills and connections needed to help an organization thrive. Some organizations consist entirely of volunteers, so members are in charge of everything, and you might need more hands to be effective. In general, boards of 7–12 people are often a good size. Make a reasoned evaluation of your ideal board size based on what you want to accomplish. Are board meetings effective, and do people participate? Each organization is different. It is crucial to maintain a "bench" of people whom you would like to invite to join the board, so that when people cycle off, you'll have ready replacements that have been vetted. Board recruitment is a constant process.

Regardless of the size or composition of your board, there are some things that will help you to be effective:

- **Boundaries on behavior.** Undefined boundaries can be as debilitating as undefined expectations. Solve the issues before they become problems. Clarify the roles of the staff and board in program areas, appropriate behavior at board meetings, and due dates for assignments.
- **Leadership**. An effective board chair is vital. See the next chapter!
- **A well-planned schedule.** Establish the right number of meetings per year. As we've pointed out before, some boards meet only once or twice a year, while others meet every month. Some have committees that meet regularly, or in the off months when there aren't regular board

meetings. If building a rapport among board members is important (and it usually is), you must have meetings frequently enough to establish those relationships. Schedule your meetings for the entire year in advance to maximize attendance.

- **Effective meetings.** You can have a great group of people, but their patience will wear thin if meetings are not well organized and well run. Show members respect by treating their time as valuable! See chapter nine for tips on how to have an effective meeting.

What you can do

- Take charge of your learning. Many states have local and online resources that offer training in areas you want to learn more about.
- Learn as much as you can about your organization's programs and how your organization works.
- Meet key members of staff and learn from them.
- Get to know the other board members.
- Learn how to talk effectively about your organization and be a great ambassador for the mission.
- Prepare for all board and committee meetings so that the meeting time is well used and you can provide useful insights.
- Listen first. Ask lots of questions.
- When working with the executive director, put yourself in the director's position. What kind of treatment and communication would you want?
- Ask questions of friends who are on other boards to find out how things are done in other nonprofits.
- Understand what's expected of you, and then do it!

REVIEW QUESTIONS

- Based on the suggestions laid out in this chapter, are you and most of your colleagues good board members?
- Do you and your fellow board members collectively have the right sets of

skills to enable the board to provide the kind of oversight and advice that is needed?

- Are you contributing in the best way possible? Are people aware of the different skills that you could potentially contribute?
- If you have suggestions for improving the board, is there a process for you to follow?
- Do you know other people who have the skills and the temperament that is needed on this board?

6

EFFECTIVE BOARD LEADERSHIP

I f the chair of your organization is a skillful communicator and knows how to run a meeting efficiently, you already have an essential component of an effective organization.

One of the crucial relationships in any nonprofit is between the board chair and the executive director. These two people often develop a close relationship by the time they've worked together for a year or two. When things go well, the strengths of each are complemented, and the organization is much better for it. When there is tension, problems arise, especially when one or both are new to the position and inexperienced. They may not yet have clearly defined their roles or worked out how they will communicate.

Sometimes board chairs think that they are supposed to be running the organization. Sometimes the executive director thinks that the board chair is a necessary evil, someone who must be tolerated or managed so that the director can get on with the job. Being clear at the outset about the nature of this relationship is essential to avoiding problems that will fester if not addressed. Let's start with the basics. Who's the boss?

The board sets the direction for the organization and works with the executive director and senior staff to develop and approve a budget that is designed to achieve the organizational goals The executive director is in charge of implementing the programs and achieving those programmatic goals within the budget. The board evaluates the director and the organization (but does not evaluate staff), and has the ultimate responsibility for ensuring that resources are used wisely and appropriately. Technically, the whole board, not the board chair, is the boss. But the board chair, along with the executive committee, is generally given the authority on behalf of the board to work closely with the executive director.

In a good working relationship, each party understands and can rely on the other to ensure the organization's success. The board chair should be careful not to circumvent the executive director. For example, if a board chair asks a senior (or any) staff member to do something, the request could place the staff member in a difficult situation.

The board chair called a senior staff member to find out about the availability of a conference room for a retreat. There were plans to do some remodeling in the conference room, which could have been changed, though it would have been a big hassle. While on the surface this was not an unreasonable request, it should have gone through the executive director. It was difficult for the staff member to say "it's not available," because the board chair was a powerful personality. There was a lot of confusion, and the staff member had to turn to the executive director anyway to resolve things. There were hurt feelings and wasted time. Going through the executive director in the first place would have avoided that problem.

Avoid confusion by consulting the executive director first, rather than going directly to members of staff.

Communication between the board chair and executive director

When, how, and about what should the board chair and the executive director communicate? Varied needs and styles of communication make for different answers to this question. You might meet or talk weekly or monthly, you might email frequently or hardly at all. When you do leave a message, how quickly do you expect to receive a response? Are there times when you don't want to be contacted, or times of day when you're usually available? Frequency of communication depends on the tasks at hand. Is the organization engaged in a new capital campaign? Are you building the budget, doing strategic planning, learning how to work together, doing an evaluation?

The crucial element here is good communication, and there are some basic rules:

- Agree on how quickly you will respond to each other.
- Specify the method you want to use to exchange information and receive answers to questions: email, phone, or text.
- Indicate whether you are comfortable getting emails at all hours of the day and night, prefer to answer things piecemeal, as they come up, or want to receive questions in batches.
- Decide how frequently you want to have regular check-ins: once a week, or every two weeks.
- Recognize that it can take longer to build a comfortable relationship if most of your communication is virtual, rather than in person.

The board chair and the executive director are important resources for each other. Treat each other gently and wisely. Nurture each other as you would your partners in any essential relationship. Set appropriate boundaries, and be clear about expectations.

A great board chair works with the executive director when planning and facilitating board meetings. When meetings go well, it is obvious. When they go badly, it is even more obvious. Planning is key, and we've devoted the next chapter to showing you how to have an effective meeting.

Communication between the board chair and the board

The board chair needs to build relationships with the various board members and understand the skills and expertise that each person brings to the organization. Board chairs ought to be as clear and open when listening to the rest of the board as they are with the executive director. When the board members feel appreciated and listened to, their level of engagement will soar.

Julia had been on the board of a social service nonprofit for two years. The board chair was somewhat self-absorbed and insecure. Julia had a lot of technical expertise and many potentially useful connections, but the board chair considered program ideas to be "his turf" and consistently blocked Julia's ideas. Fortunately, his term was up, and a new board chair took over. She reached out to Julia, appreciated her talents and connections, and encouraged her to present some of her ideas at the next board meeting. Two of those ideas were enthusiastically received, and Julia started to have a much larger role in developing creative strategies for the nonprofit.

The board chair sets the tone of the organization, and must have the authority to negotiate when the situation calls for it.

In one case, a challenging situation arose among three different organizations working to negotiate a memorandum of understanding. Some fiery personalities were involved, but the board chair was a trained lawyer and negotiator with an exceptionally calm demeanor. Her temperament was perfectly suited to building rapport and working through the negotiations. She stayed calm when challenged, was able to keep the conversation moving, and worked hard to build consensus. Everyone was able to come to a satisfactory agreement. Without her leadership, the negotiations would probably have collapsed.

Leadership transitions

One of the biggest challenges faced by an executive director can be the transition between board chairs. An executive director who serves for ten years may have had five or six different bosses, all with their own styles, needs, strengths, challenges, timetables, and personalities. How much time does it take to get used to, and often train, the new person? Some organizations use the vice chair position for the person who will be next in line to assume the chair role in order to help support the leadership transition. Sometimes the vice chair joins the chair in the latter's one-on-one meetings with the executive director during the last six months of the chair's term.

Board chairs need to be aware, as they assume their positions, that their executive directors have grown accustomed to doing things in a particular way with the previous chairs. When new chairs come in and start doing things differently, tensions will arise. Being gentle and collaborative will make life easier and more productive for everyone. Executive directors also need to remember that board chairs have their own styles of leadership, and they need freedom to implement that. Above all, they must talk to and listen to each other, and allow time to build a good relationship.

Transitions often create challenges, as all involved struggle to set boundaries, define roles, establish a communication style, and develop a good working relationship. A first-time board chair without good transition skills can take months to sort this out. Similarly, a new director can experience frustration when the roles, boundaries, and authority of the chair are unclear.

Appropriate length of time as board chair

Two common scenarios are:

1. No one wants to be the board chair, so someone who doesn't really want to do it agrees to take on the task, but doesn't have much energy or skill for doing it.
2. The board chair wants the position for life and won't let go. If your organization has clear term limits for board members and officers, you will be less likely to run into the problem of trying to oust a chair who is reluctant to depart.

A board chair of a small organization also served as the unpaid business manager. It was a great organization. He loved the work and was effective as the chair. It seemed to make sense for him to continue in both roles. He did this for 12 years, until shortly before he left the board. Even though he was effective, the organization would have been in better shape had he separated the business manager work from the board chair position. He could then have stepped down as chair and mentored someone else into the business manager position. Instead, when he left, the organization lost two key roles at the same time, and it was traumatic for the nonprofit. The organization also had to recast the budget to hire a business manager to provide services that it had previously received for free.

Usually, a board chair will serve for two years, and some organizations allow for a repeat term to maximize the relationship between the chair and the executive director. In most circumstances, two years is a good term limit. The board may vote to renew the term if things are going well, the current chair is interested. It also depends on the availability of others to serve in the position. The board should take the time to do a thoughtful evaluation of how things are going and make a reasoned decision. A clear process for succession avoids the problem of an overbearing board chair hanging on to power. One of the leading reasons that executive directors give for leaving is a difficult relationship with the board or the board chair.

Extra responsibilities of the board chair

- As with all leadership roles, the board chair should be good at delegating tasks and communicating clearly with other board members.
- The board chair is often responsible for signing corporate documents and being a public face of the organization.
- It can be helpful and persuasive to have the board chair join the executive director in a meeting with a foundation to show that the board is involved in and supportive of that project.
- If there is a public problem or an exciting new project, the board chair might join the executive director in talking to the media.

Responsibilities of other officers

State law, not federal law, determines which officers a nonprofit must have. Most states require a president or chair of the board as well as a secretary. In some states, this can be the same person. Check with your state's department of justice if you need clarification. Your organization's bylaws should outline what roles are mandated for your nonprofit.

- **Vice-chair.** We discussed above preparing someone for the board chair position. Some board chairs delegate a range of tasks to a vice-chair. Make this an active role! Turn the occasional meeting over to the vice-chair to participate in the formation of agendas. Meet afterward and give feedback. By assigning tasks, you can ease the load on the chair, give meaning to the vice-chair role and experience to the person occupying it, and lead toward a smoother transition when that person takes over.
- **Secretary.** This is generally a required position for a nonprofit. The secretary is responsible for making sure that minutes are taken and saved, although sometimes the task of taking minutes is assumed by a staff member or other board member. Some documents may require the secretary's signature.
- **Treasurer.** This is an important oversight position that can add clarity and perspective to the board's financial understanding. The treasurer should be someone who knows enough about finances to understand the financial reports and deliver a reliable evaluation to the board. Many organizations also have a finance committee, usually led by the treasurer, that reviews the books and any annual audit.

Board committees

Board committees can help increase the board's efficiency. Some organizations are able to reduce the number of meetings because the committees do effective work in between board meetings. The number and kind of board committees needed varies greatly from one organization to another. You should have clarity about both the authority and the responsibilities of each committee, and a means of evaluating their effectiveness. For temporary committee work, it can be helpful to set up short-term task forces with a specific goal. Once that goal is accomplished, the task force can disband.

Each committee should have a charter or agreement that outlines its overall purpose, who will chair the committee, how many members must be board members, whether or not non-board members are allowed to serve on the committee, the frequency of the meetings, the length of time that committee members will serve, the process for reporting the committee's findings, and decision-making authority.

Some committees continue meeting beyond their usefulness. Each committee should have a yearly review to decide if they are still useful and if they should change their role. Let's look at the most traditional committees:

- **Executive committee**. Usually, this consists of the officers of the board. Some nonprofits have board meetings every other month, and they have an executive committee meeting in the off-months, with the committee empowered to make decisions between board meetings. Some have an executive committee that meets only when an emergency or a major issue arises whose resolution is better handled by a small group than by the whole board. What's critical is that the power and authority of the executive committee be clear. What can they decide without a full board vote? The scope of duties should be laid out explicitly in writing. Without a clear scope of duties, confusion and frustration, if not outright rebellion, may result from decisions made by the executive committee. We've seen a number of instances where the executive committee of a nonprofit has made decisions that the board did not support, and where the board did not believe the decisions were within the purview of the executive committee. It can be difficult to recover from this.
- **Finance and audit committee**. This group often includes the treasurer, the executive director, and one or two other people who may be board members or community members with needed expertise. Financial experts on the committee should understand the differences between

nonprofit and for-profit accounting. Sometimes, for-profit financial experts don't recognize their own limitations when it comes to nonprofit finance. It's different! The members of your finance committee must truly understand the committee's role and the complexities of nonprofit finances. Make sure that suitable training is available. For the audit, the committee is charged with oversight of the audit process, including selecting the audit firm. If you are not currently doing an audit, you might occasionally assemble a task force to examine whether it is time to do one, or contract for an outside financial review.

- **Development or fundraising committee**. Almost every nonprofit has to raise funds. The traditional role of the development committee is to make sure that the organization has a development plan for the year and that the plan is followed. The development director or the executive director will turn to this group for advice, for connections, and for input, and sometimes to participate in meetings with potential funders. Members of the development committee might be people with connections to local foundations or people of wealth. Don't make the mistake of thinking that the development committee has sole responsibility for raising the funds that the organization needs. All board members participate, in one way or another, in fundraising.

- **Board development committee**. This important committee assists in maintaining a pipeline of potential board members and helps to vet them. Committee members should be well versed in the skills being sought as well as the culture and style of meetings that you want to maintain. As we've mentioned before, one contentious board member can ruin the dynamic of a well-functioning group. The opposite can also be true—one great board member can shift the dynamics in a positive direction. This committee can also be charged with the ongoing training and development of board members, including the annual board member assessments. We talk more about how to recruit board members in chapter 16.

REVIEW QUESTIONS

- Is the role of the board chair clearly defined? In particular, is the chair's relationship with the executive director clearly articulated and understood?
- Are the terms and responsibilities of board officers clearly laid out?
- Is it clear how the nominating process for new officer positions works?
- Is there a smooth process for the transition from one board chair to another?
- Is there a charter or a clear outline of how committees work, who the members are, how long they serve, what decision-making responsibility they have, and what will be expected of the committee?
- Does the board regularly review which committees it has and decide if they are necessary, if they should be changed, or if new ones are needed?
- Has the board eliminated any committees that are no longer adding value?

7

HOW TO HAVE PRODUCTIVE BOARD MEETINGS

Some board meetings are dry, but they're well organized, and a lot of things get done. Other meetings are energizing, with great chemistry among the people and inspiring conversations that enhance the connection to the mission. Some are creative, as new projects are explored and envisioned. Everyone leaves the meeting feeling excited to continue the work.

Then there are the *other* meetings: the no-fun, ineffective meetings that leave board members fuming, or asleep. How many of us have sat through someone reading a report that could have been sent out in advance? Other meetings get bogged down in discussions about inconsequential things, leaving no time to address a looming existential crisis.

One basic way to evaluate the effectiveness of a meeting is to ask, Did we accomplish something important that wouldn't have been accomplished if we hadn't had a meeting? Did it make a difference to me or to the organization that I was there?

Structures and tactics that lead to an effective board meeting

- Send out an agenda, reports (of the executive director, board chair, and any committees), and financials at least one week before the meeting. Give members a chance to look things over and digest the information so that they'll be able to ask productive questions and understand the issues. If you have questions or feedback that you want addressed, highlight those in the report so that people can think about them in advance.

- Start and end meetings on time. This shows respect for the people present. If you habitually wait for one or two people to arrive, and start meetings 10 minutes late, everyone else will start arriving late, too.

- The agenda should be clear, with realistic time frames associated with each item. Agendas are normally developed by the board chair and executive director, with input from other board members. Too often, items that will require 20 minutes are assigned five minutes so that everything fits into the agenda. If your meetings always run over, you need to rethink your facilitation skills or your agendas.

- Clearly mark on the agenda any action items that will require a vote. This helps people focus on issues that need a decision. The wording of the action items should clearly state who will do them, what will be done, when it will happen, and how it will be reported back.

- Treat one another with respect. Immediately and politely call out inappropriate or disrespectful behavior. Often, people are unaware or unthinking when they act badly, so gently confronting people can be worthwhile.

- Schedule board meetings for the entire year in advance. It is best to set a specific time (the third Thursday of every month, for example) so that people have a plan for the year.

- Present financials that are clear and up to date, with concerns or questions highlighted. Give people time to ask questions.

- Provide translation, if needed, for any board members for whom English is a second language. If you have monolingual speakers of other languages on your board, consider holding some meetings in their language, so that all board members can experience what it is like to participate through the use of a translator.

- Try to learn something new about the organization at every meeting.

- Send out any committee reports in advance. Use the board meeting for discussion and action items. *Whatever you do, don't read reports at the meeting!!* This is one of the ultimate time and energy killers.
- Arrive a bit early, and stay a bit late. This improves the chances of starting on time and gives you the opportunity to get to know some of your fellow board members.
- Be sure that the secretary or notetaker has a good system that records all important information without recapping every discussion. Review how the notes are taken at each meeting until you develop the kind of board notes that you want; then, make sure you stick to that format. Don't assume that the format you've always used is the best or only way possible.
- Develop a process for documenting and storing board decisions so that they are easily accessed for the next three years when a question arises.

Some organizations use Robert's Rules of Order, which lays out meeting protocols very clearly, if somewhat rigidly. Many people find that the following basic rules effectively foster respectful behavior:

- Don't interrupt or talk over someone.
- Listen to what people are saying, rather than plan what you will say next.
- If you normally talk a lot, talk less. If you rarely talk, speak up.
- Don't weigh in on every topic. Only comment when you have something meaningful to add.
- For each topic, ascertain whether the goal is simply discussion and understanding, or whether a decision is needed.
- Come to the meeting prepared: read reports in advance and think about questions that you have. Too often, people read material for the first time at the meeting. This slows things down and frequently leads to unhelpful comments that are off the cuff, rather than thoughtful.
- If any board members have trouble keeping up with the conversation (because of language, hearing issues, shyness, lack of familiarity with the subject, or some other reason), check in with them, and make sure that they understand the conversation and have the chance to speak.

- Don't be afraid to have spaces of silence in a conversation.
- If your meetings are virtual, don't assume that people know how to communicate effectively in this way. Provide clear guidelines in order to get full participation. Recognize that it may take practice and guidance to have effective video-conference meetings.

I remember an engaging board meeting at an organization that supports women in Zimbabwe by helping them sell their art in the United States. The board faced a big decision about whether to send a US artist to Zimbabwe for two months to work with the women. The seven board members had all received the executive director's proposal beforehand, and we knew that we would be making a decision that night. I thought it would be better to use the money to expand the artist center in Weya, and we couldn't do both.

After listening to comments from the other board members, I shifted my position, recognizing the advantages of having a guest artist visit, building relationships with the women, and helping to understand what it was that they really needed. I left the meeting with a sense of excitement and exhilaration about the quality of our board debate and the project we were going to undertake.

Group norms

Another important aspect of effective meetings is clearly understanding your group norms. Every group has a way of operating. Often these norms are informal rules of behavior. The rules may vary greatly from one group to another, and they may shift over time, especially as some people leave and new board members join. There isn't a right or a wrong way, but to be an effective member of the group, you need to understand how the group operates. When everyone agrees on the rules, it is surprising how smooth and energizing board meetings can be. And of course, there are times when the norms themselves may be the problem.

One executive committee was having an intense discussion about the future of one of the facilities, but the group had gotten off topic, complaining about one of the city commissioners. When I, as the executive director, suggested that in the interest of time, we should refocus on the facility in question, one of the other board members said, "It's the board chair's job to run the meeting, not yours." I was quite taken aback. But I also learned that I needed an alternative method of getting the conversation back on track.

Many group norms will be easy to spot if you are paying attention, and by the end of your first board meeting, you will likely be aware of most of them. Sometimes, you'll get conflicting information, as norms can shift, be understood in different ways, or be ignored. If you're unsure, ask for clarification.

One member of a board that I joined was always late. Always! Other board members grew used to this, and eventually, they just started the meeting on time, and when the "late person" arrived, they would backtrack and catch him up on the conversation. At the third board meeting, even though I was relatively new, I waited for an appropriate time and asked, "I wonder if we should change the time of the meeting to 15 minutes later so that we could start on time and not have to backtrack at every meeting?" People began to talk about their expectations and their frustrations. The chronically late person didn't realize the effect that he was having on everyone else. No one had talked to him about it. He apologized and promised to start arriving on time. We didn't need to shift the meeting time.

To understand the group norms, you may want to have a conversation with your "board buddy", the executive director or the board chair. Ask about any protocols or ways of behaving that seem to be unique to the organization. If the norms just don't work for you, you should carefully consider whether you want to be a part of that group.

One board I observed had 40 members. They met only once a year, so the first hour of the two-hour meeting included introductions of all the members present. The board chair then made some opening comments, after which they voted on new members and board officer positions. Then they reviewed the annual audit and adjourned for cocktails. The meeting was expressly designed to avoid any substantive issues or discussions. A board member told me that it was the same as it had been since he had first joined thirty years earlier. I helped a few new board members understand the culture so that they could determine if this was an appropriate board for them to join.

The following are some of the questions that you may want to consider. Ask someone on the board if the answers aren't immediately apparent to you.

- Is there a dress code, and if so, how closely is it followed?
- How much latitude is there for showing up late to meetings or leaving early?
- Do people eat or drink during the meetings?
- Is alcohol served at board meetings?
- What is the group's comfort level when faced with conflict or difficult conversations?
- Is the board chair clearly in charge of running the meeting, or is the meeting more free-wheeling?
- Do you get through everything on the agenda on time, or do you often have to extend meetings?
- Are most items rubber stamped, or is there genuine discussion and debate?
- Is there a set time allotted for each discussion topic? Is it adhered to?
- How much do people contribute to the conversation? Do certain people speak on every subject, whether or not they have something to add?
- Are quiet members given a specific opportunity to speak?
- Are people respectful of each other?
- Can members add something to the agenda at any point, or is there a clear protocol?

- Do staff members attend? If they do, how much interaction between board members and staff members is appropriate?
- Do certain people dominate the meeting?
- Do meetings start and end on time?
- Are the next steps and timing of any action items clear?
- Does it make a difference that you were there?

A board chair I worked with typically got so caught up in discussions that she lost track of time and the agenda. Every meeting ran over time, and several important agenda items kept getting deferred. Eventually, she asked another board member to facilitate the meetings. This allowed the board chair to fully participate in the discussions, without also having to keep track of the agenda. The other board member was great at running the meetings and keeping the group moving forward. She enjoyed the chance to have a leadership role without the additional responsibilities of board chair.

Board meetings should be useful, instructive, and, most of the time, enjoyable. Everyone has something else that they could be doing, so make the best use of valuable time. Board meetings can inspire people, help them feel valued, and give them the tools to be effective in their roles. When you leave a board meeting, you want to feel uplifted and energized to help the organization thrive.

REVIEW QUESTIONS

- Do board meetings feel productive? If not, why not?
- Do you understand the culture of the board?
- Do you know how to participate and be effective?
- Do you look forward to the next board meeting? If not, what would make that happen?
- Are you actively making sure that board meetings are effective and productive?

8

ORGANIZATIONAL AND BOARD POLICIES

The IRS has a number of organizational and board policy requirements related to legal, ethical, and practical concerns. Individual states have others. It is easy to let these things slide, but policies require attention and regular updating. While many policies are recommended, rather than required, your tax return (990) specifically asks you to confirm that certain policies are in place. Nonprofit tax returns are public information, so anyone looking at them can see if you have complied. Equally important are the board discussion and explanation of each policy, which ensure that everyone clearly understands the meaning and implementation.

Let's look at the most important policies first.

Conflict of interest policy

When you file your 990 nonprofit tax return, the IRS will ask if you have a conflict of interest policy. You are allowed to say no, and there will be no penalty. That shouldn't make you think that you don't need one. Why?

While the federal government doesn't insist that nonprofits have such a policy, some states do. New York, for example, requires you to have a conflict of interest policy in place. Because this varies from state to state, you need to check your state's rules.

More importantly, when you read about a problematic nonprofit with bad publicity, it often stems from a conflict of interest. As a board member, you are required to put the good of the organization above your own, so it is important to know exactly what you are agreeing to.

Having a clear conflict of interest policy, signed each year by every board member, clarifies your nonprofit's rules. As a board member, you cannot take advantage of your board relationship to the detriment of the organization. This doesn't mean that you can't do work for your nonprofit, or even get paid for it, but it means that certain rules must be followed regarding fairness, disclosure, and recusing yourself when your self-interest might be involved. Everyone on the board should disclose any potential conflicts of interest; then, the board should follow a procedure that allows the group to discuss the matter and make a decision without the member whose interests conflict being in the room.

If you do an internet search for "conflict of interest policy," you will find ample examples that you can customize to create a suitable policy for your organization.

Harassment policy

Even if your organization is not legally required to have a harassment policy, it is highly recommended. Whether or not the organization has a written policy, you are still responsible for prohibiting, preventing, and effectively addressing any issues of harassment. A clear, effective harassment policy that is openly talked about at both the board and the staff levels sends a strong message that no types of harassment will be allowed in your organization. Your policy should outline what is meant by the terms used and what steps should be followed should someone experience or believe that they have experienced harassment. The purpose is twofold. Not only does the policy provide your organization with a way to handle problems that arise, but also simply having the policy may help the organization avoid problems in the first place by clearly articulating prohibited behaviors.

A number of years ago, a college we worked with had a dean who was acting inappropriately around staff. He was also designated as the person to go to with harassment issues, making it difficult to know how to report this and get help. One of his staff members put up with his advances for a few years before she found a trustworthy person to talk to without losing her job. The dean ended up getting fired, and an effective policy was finally put into place, but it was a long, costly, and painful lesson for everyone involved.

Non-discrimination policy

For reasons similar to those described in the harassment policy, we strongly recommend that you have a clear non-discrimination policy. Be straight-forward about how your organization defines discrimination and what steps a person should take if they feel they have been discriminated against. If everyone clearly understands what constitutes discrimination, they will be less likely to engage in discriminatory behavior in the first place.

Here is an example of a nondiscrimination policy:

The [Institution Name] is committed to diversity and to equal opportunity employment. [Institution Name] does not discriminate on the basis of race, creed, color, ethnicity, national origin, religion, sex, sexual orientation, gender identity and expression, age, height, weight, physical or mental ability (including HIV status), veteran status, military obligations, or marital status. This policy applies to hiring, internal promotions, training, opportunities for advancement, and terminations and applies to all [Institution Name] employees, volunteers, members, clients, and contractors."

All board members and staff should have a thorough orientation about the many ways that discrimination and harassment appear in and affect organizations. Sometimes people are not even aware that their actions are problematic until it is pointed out to them.

Whistleblower policy

In 2002, Congress enacted the *Sarbanes-Oxley Act*, to increase corporate accountability after Enron and Worldcom dissolved in a matter of months following their financial scandals. Federal law prohibits all corporations, including nonprofits, from retaliating against employees who "blow the whistle" on their employer's accounting practices. Additionally, over 45 different states have enacted laws to protect whistleblowers from retaliation at the workplace. An effective policy outlines how a whistleblower is protected, how and with whom to issue a complaint, and how to manage confidentiality.

Record retention and destruction policy

In a time of proliferating information (and the multitude of ways that documents are shared), it is essential to have rules written down about record retention and destruction. Your organization must keep some records forever, and others for varying amounts of time. If the IRS comes calling, and you have thrown out important documents that you were supposed to have, you might be in trouble. Moreover, if you need to look back for any reason to see when and how a decision was made, a document retention policy ensures that important documents are still available. There is no one-size-fits-all policy for record retention, because state laws vary. In general, though, the following documents should be kept forever:

- Articles of incorporation and your organization's determination letter from the IRS (and any other correspondence regarding the letter)
- Bylaws—and any subsequent changes to those bylaws—as well as any corporate resolutions
- Year-end financial statements, as well as any audits and letters relating

   to the audits
- Board meeting minutes
- Copies of the organization's 990 forms (the yearly tax return)
- Insurance policies (some policies cover a specific time period that is protected forever for anything that happened during that period)
- Personnel files

Develop a clear policy that outlines which documents your organization will save, for how long, and where and how those records will be kept. Always keep electronic copies of these documents in case the originals are destroyed or lost. There are lots of stories of former founders and board chairs who, having passed away, leave a box containing the original documents in their basements, to be thrown out by unsuspecting family members.

An effective retention policy also specifies who is responsible for implementing the policy, and when they will do it. Records that don't need to be kept permanently should be reviewed annually and unnecessary ones destroyed.

Other things for which you might want to have a policy:

Your organization may benefit from having other policies depending on such factors as the size of your nonprofit, whether you have an endowment, and the scope and type of your assets. The board should review the list every year or two to make sure that the organization has all of the necessary policies in place and that they are up-to-date.

Maintenance (e.g. policies for spending from facility reserves)

Does your nonprofit own any real estate or expensive machinery or equipment? Does it have a fund set aside for repairs or replacement? Does the organization put aside money for depreciation, or ignore it to break even for the year? Having a maintenance policy increases the chances that you will address problems before they arise, and enable you to pay for the big ones when they do occur.

Endowment or reserve policy

If your organization has an endowment, you need clear, written policies about how those funds can and will be used. The IRS has rules about the maximum percentage of the endowment that your organization is allowed to use on a yearly basis, but that doesn't mean you should use the maximum allowed. Your organization's policy should specify how much of those funds may be used in any given year, as well as when, if ever, you will make exceptions. Reserves (as opposed to a formal endowment) don't usually have those legal restrictions, but your organization should have clear policies about how and when you will use them.

Investments

For invested funds (whether reserves or endowment), your organization should have a plan that clearly indicates how they are invested, who is empowered to make changes to the plan, and how often the plan is reviewed. If you have an investment advisor, meet regularly. Too often, invested funds either languish or lose money, because no one is keeping an eye on what is done with them.

Gift acceptance policy

Gifts are wonderful, but free is sometimes very expensive.

> One organization accepted a parcel of land without carefully analyzing what the offer included. They were on the hook for expensive mainte-nance and weren't allowed to sell it for many years. When they finally did sell, there were many hoops to jump through. This was a gift they should have refused.

Carefully assess gifts that are offered, and graciously decline when they don't meet your organization's needs or have too many strings attached. Having a good policy in place that outlines what kinds of gifts you will and won't accept makes the decision easier. Have the conversation with the board before your organization accepts a gift, not after it becomes an issue.

You may also want to articulate a naming policy within the gift acceptance policies that spells out the size of gift and other considerations— perhaps the honor of naming a room, building, or other asset belonging to the organization.

> *For a capital campaign, one organization decided to offer benches with donors' names on them. They did not spell out how long the benches were to be in place or any kind of maintenance funds to keep the benches in good repair. The families expected that their loved ones' names would be on the benches forever. Years later, when the organization had to remove the benches due to age and disrepair, the families that had given to the organization were dismayed.*

Executive director compensation

How does your nonprofit determine the executive director's compensation? Is it based on a knowledge of comparable salaries at nonprofits of similar size in your area? When an underpaid director leaves, the organization may have to increase the salary substantially to hire another person with less experience and expertise than the departing director. Sometimes, the departing director would have stayed if the organization had offered fairer treatment and compensation. With a policy in place, it is also easier to respond to an executive director's request for a salary increase.

Diversity, equity, inclusion, and anti-racism (DEI).

We have a lot of work to do in our nonprofits to fix the systemic inequities and injustices that have accrued in our society over multiple generations.

Many boards recognize both a responsibility to strive for greater diversity, equity, and inclusion, as well as the many benefits and opportunities that a diverse staff and a diversity of opinion can bring to an organization. More and more funders are also requiring progress in relation to diversity, equity, and inclusion; and potential employees (and board members) are looking to see evidence of the organization's support for anti-racist efforts and DEI before they apply for a position. It is crucial to develop policies about DEI, and to recognize that attitudes cannot be changed merely by developing a policy. A deep understanding of and commitment to these issues is necessary to truly make a change within your organization. This includes making a commitment to these efforts at the board level.

Many foundations recognize the need for support in this area and may sponsor training and provide funds to hire consultants to help you develop policies and make progress in this area. See chapter 10 for more information about diversity, equity, inclusion and anti-racism.

Executive director's authority

Are the board and the director clear about what authority the director has and when the board should be consulted or informed? Up to what dollar amount can an executive director initiate a new contract? Should it be $2,000 or $20,000? What about signing a ten-year lease? Can she hire a new development director who will need to work closely with the board to be successful? Is it okay to fire a long-time employee without consulting the board? Clarifying expectations up front minimizes problems that may arise.

Form and content of board minutes (committee minutes)

Specify the format your board will use to record minutes, as well as when and how they are reviewed and approved. Decide where they are stored, in what form, and for how long. Minutes that record every detail of the meeting will probably never be read and reviewed. Come up with a format that most people agree is useful.

Board motions and resolutions

Effective tracking of board resolutions is a perennial problem for most organizations. The resolutions get buried in meeting minutes, and most groups don't have the patience to review ten years' worth of minutes to see if an issue ever came up and how it was resolved. One way to track resolutions is to keep a separate notebook (which can be online), in which you chronologically record motions under certain topics, such as board structure, staffing issues, financial decisions, and banking votes. Create your own system, and expand it as new topic areas arise. This collection of resolutions is another way to help orient new board members to the decisions made previously by the organization.

Board member/chair tenure

Often, your organization's bylaws will dictate board terms (both their length, and the number of terms a person may serve) for members and officers. Check to see what is already in place. If there are no written rules, then the organization should set up a policy. When board members or officers stay too long, they can become a problem. Without a policy in place (and sometimes even with one), it can be difficult to remove someone from the board. Your bylaws should outline the process by which you would do this—usually, by a vote of some percentage of the board. On rare occasions, a board member may do something illegal or in violation of your organization's rules or norms. If there is clear evidence of this, you can simply follow the organization's established procedures to remove the person from the board. More often, the problem is that a board member is obstructionist, unpleasant to be around, or has a very different vision of where your nonprofit should be focusing its energy and direction. These are difficult situations, and setting policies in place before they are needed can facilitate the removal of a problematic board member when such circumstances arise.

I joined a board where one long-term member had started to feel proprietary about the organization. He felt he should be the deciding person on all issues and shut down any conversation that explored ideas contrary to his vision. I met with the board chair and asked if anyone had ever talked to this member about how his behavior was affecting the group. "No, we've talked about how annoying it is, but we've just sort of put up with "John" because he's been there so long and he doesn't take criticism well." I suggested we check in with the executive committee and get together with John to talk to him. We were polite, but very direct with him about how his actions were affecting the group and that he needed to modify them. We informed him that we would be reviewing our rules of behavior at board meetings.

We outlined our new agreement for how discussions would be handled and the policy enforced at the next board meeting. There was a vote to ensure official agreement from everyone. After some hesitation, even John voted for it. It was still challenging, but things gradually improved, and people started enjoying meetings again. But if it hadn't gotten better, we were clear about expectations, and it would have been easier to vote him off the board if that had been necessary.

REVIEW QUESTIONS

- Have all members of the board seen and reviewed your 990?
- Do you have a written conflict of interest policy and has everyone signed a copy?
- Has the board reviewed the policies in this chapter to determine which ones your organization should have in place?
- Does your organization regularly monitor and enforce compliance with all policies?
- Do all board members have an easy and systematic way to access board minutes and previous board decisions?
- Does your organization have a diversity, equity, and inclusion policy, and, if so, are you serious about implementing it?

9

MISSION, VISION, AND VALUES

O ne of the crucial jobs of any board is to shape and advance the mission, vision, and values of an organization. An understanding of what each of these terms means for your nonprofit will help clarify what the organization, and you as a board member, want to accomplish. Unfortunately, these words often produce a lot of confusion and misunderstanding. The word "mission" by itself is a landmine of multiple possible interpretations. Does it mean purpose, goals, activities, strategies? Does it describe the "how," or only the "what"? Should it also specify "who" your nonprofit intends to serve ? Is a vision different from a mission? Are the values personal behaviors and beliefs, or are they broader organizational values? What is strategy, anyway? Because these words can be defined in so many ways, this chapter will help you to understand and apply them to your nonprofit work.

As a board member, you should expect clarity around:

- The values of the organization (who you, as an organization, are, and what drives the organization's actions).
- The purpose of the organization (why the organization exists).
- The mission/goal of the organization (what you, as an organization, are doing).

- The vision (what the world will look like if you're successful).
- The strategy of the organization (how you are doing it, when it will be accomplished, and where the work will take place).
- The organization's audience (whom you serve).

You can call these things whatever you want, but it is important to understand the *who, why, what, how, when, where,* and *for whom* of your organization so that your recommendations can be aligned with the vision of the organization.

I joined an organization whose mission was "championing the en-trepreneurial spirit." Despite the catchy nature of this phrase, it wasn't very helpful as a mission statement. To be useful, a mission statement should provide a context for deciding which programs to pursue. We realized that championing entrepreneurs was really more of a purpose. It defined why we existed as an organization, but our mission was to create programs that would reach 1000 middle-stage business owners over the next five years and help them to develop plans for the growth of those businesses. This clarification energized our program staff and our board.

Values should be the core of your organization's existence. You should be willing to fight for them. For example, many organizations list integrity as a value, but unless something about your organization's approach to integrity differentiates you from other organizations, it's probably just a generic value, like providing great service and being financially responsible. To be more helpful, your organization's values should be something you truly and actively believe in, something on the forefront of your consciousness whenever you think about the organization. Ask yourself what behavioral values really set your organization apart. Is your organization playful? Humble? Empowering of employees? Committed to diversity? If your organization is all about command and control, own it. Narrow down the top five core values and then commit to bringing everyone in the organization around to exhibiting those values.

Purpose answers the question of why your organization exists. For a nonprofit, this is perhaps the most important issue to clarify. Why is your nonprofit here? What would the world be missing without it? On some level, nearly all nonprofits are working to make the world a better place. Are you giving a voice to the voiceless, doing right by future generations, making the world more beautiful, fairer, and more diverse? Why are you doing all this work? The answer is probably much bigger than a service that you provide or a product that you sell. Make sure you are clear about your organization's purpose and then articulate it well so others understand it as well.

Mission is the goal that orients the organization. Mission is sending someone to the moon and back again. It has a clear finish line, and it compels you to do things that push you toward achievement of that goal. In 1969, going to the moon and back was the mission, but it required huge investments in education, scientific research, and infrastructure to achieve. Mission should have metrics attached, so that you'll know when you have succeeded and can set a new mission. A mission should inspire and stretch you to achieve it. The mission should align with your nonprofit's values and purpose.

Vision is how you see a future in which your nonprofit has succeeded in accomplishing its mission. For example: "Our vision is a world where music-making knows no boundaries," or, "Our vision is a world in which all people have the opportunity of a safe place to live."

Strategy sets out how your nonprofit will accomplish the mission. How will you get to the moon? You do it by organizing staff, securing funding, promoting the project, meeting with stakeholders, performing research, developing mathematics to know where you will actually land, and a thousand other things. How will you bring safe drinking water to 100,000 people in Mali and Niger? By raising money, designing solar-powered filtration systems, recruiting volunteers to dig safe latrines that keep waste out of water supplies.

Whatever your organization's approach to achieving the mission, all of the systems you will use, all of the marketing you will deploy, all of the fundraising you will conduct, all of the hiring in which you will engage...these elements will be your strategy. As a board member, you may not be involved in developing the strategies, but you should review them to make sure that they are moving the organization toward the goal that its mission has defined. Be certain that your organization's strategies align with its values and purpose. When correctly designed, the values, purpose, mission, and strategies all work as a unified whole to orient the energy of the organization's staff toward some greater good. The board agrees on this vision and assists the organization with relationships and financial support.

Audience is who you will be addressing. It is not necessarily just your clients or customers; it might also include other providers, funders, or the general public.

Let's look at a weak and then a strong example to see how clarity and alignment can empower a nonprofit and how a comprehensive vision can help the organization set its direction.

Preschool Northwest—a therapeutic preschool		
	Weak	Stronger
Values	• Honesty • Integrity • Collaboration • Financial Stability	• Offer equal access to clients, regardless of ability to pay. • Approach work in a collaborative spirit. Support the child, the parents, and the providers. • Promote happiness by creating a nurturing environment. • Be authentic. • Recognize individual needs in a holistic way.
Purpose	We help children in need.	Improve the lives of families with children who have disabilities.
Mission	We provide home-based services to children with severe disabilities, and we work with parents to help them cope with caring for a child with disabilities.	By 2025, we will have transformed how children with disabilities throughout Oregon receive educational services.
Vision	We want to help disabled children.	Our vision is a world where children with disabilities and their families have the best possible life that caring and transformative services can provide.

Strategies	• Set up counseling services. • Solicit donations that can support parents who can't afford to pay. • Find other like-minded counselors who can provide services. • Engage in ongoing planning and evaluation in partnership with the community.	• Hold therapy sessions in a residential setting. • Raise funds to pay for scholarships to make sure all families can utilize services. • Hire therapists who follow a "no-fault" philosophy. • Create a learning community so that everyone is aware of and actively involved in using the latest ideas in the therapeutic field. • Expand outreach by partnering with public schools as a source of referrals. • Document and actively share our work and our results with other groups serving people and families with disabilities.
Audience	Parents and children	Families with children who have one or more disabilities. We also seek to reach other disability providers.

The **values** in the weak version are good, but rather generic; they don't help you know what to do. Similarly, the **purpose** is general. All children have needs. Which ones will your organization help? And the **mission** describes what the organization does, not a goal that can be accomplished. "We provide services to children" is not a mission, it's a statement of activity. The **vision** and **strategies** are also general, making it harder to know if you have succeeded.

On the other hand, the **values** in the stronger version give you more guidance about how you should act and what to expect from others. The **purpose** is more specific, and lets people know that your organization is concerned for the families as well as the children. The **mission** compels the organization to execute a series of actions that are designed to help the organization accomplish a broad goal. And it follows with a **vision** of the world we would like to see and **strategies** that if completed will assure that the mission is accomplished. Finally we have much more clarity about the **audience** we are serving.

In the second example, the intent is much larger than just helping a handful of families. Your organization will transform how all families receive services across the state. That changes how you do your work and how you collaborate with others.

To sum up: A mission is not a marketing slogan. It's a goal that helps your organization move toward fulfilling its purpose. A purpose statement, meanwhile, may sound similar to another organization's purpose. Purpose statements are inspirational, not differentiating. Strategy—how you do it—is what will differentiate your organization from others.

As you review all of these statements, keep in mind that basic question: Are we providing the public benefit in the best way possible? Being clear about your organization's mission, vision, and strategies should help you feel energized and centered on the great work that you can accomplish.

REVIEW QUESTIONS

- Do you understand the organization well enough to be able to articulate the mission in your own words?
- Do you have at least two personal stories that compellingly show why this is an important mission to you and why your organization offers a good solution to this problem?
- Can you share the top three initiatives or programs of the organization?
- Does the mission align with the values and the purpose?
- Is the mission something that can be accomplished with a clear outcome and within a reasonable timeframe?
- Do your organization's values help you distinguish who you should hire or not hire?

10

DIVERSITY, EQUITY, INCLUSION, AND ANTI-RACISM

N onprofits have an important role to play in building awareness and taking action towards increasing diversity, equity, and inclusion (often referred to as DEI) and dismantling systemic racism. This awareness expands understanding of how racism affects everyone, demonstrating the need for anti-racism efforts to begin to address long-standing inequalities and misconceptions. Board members have a responsibility to take a leadership role in these efforts. To bring about meaningful change, the board must come to a common understanding with staff regarding the nonprofit's approach to DEI and anti-racism efforts. Many people struggle to understand exactly what these terms mean, so definition is an essential first step before implementation of policies and structures. Organizations looking for ideas and strategies to address pressing inequities can find ample resources in books, trainings, and the recommendations of peer-organizations. Including people who've been historically excluded from organizational structures and positions of power is equally important and requires thoughtful implementation. This exploration can uncover the richness and opportunity that comes with incorporating diverse viewpoints and different ways of working together.

Changing deeply ingrained, often unconscious, beliefs is challenging and emotional. Invariably, there will be different levels of support for and resistance to addressing these issues. Done well, it can have transformational effects on your work and your organization. Done poorly, it can create chaos and lasting scars. Open communication, a plan, and a willingness to be vulnerable are integral to having a chance for success. This chapter should provide a basic understanding of some of the issues associated with diversity, equity, inclusion, and anti-racism.

Let's start with some definitions

Diversity in an organization or workplace usually includes differences in race, ethnicity, gender, age, religion, disability, sexual orientation, gender identity and expression, socioeconomic status, class, language, education, values, and styles of communication. This is often extended to include differences in physical appearance, cultural background, lived experiences, and ways of viewing the world. When we talk about diversity, we also mean that these differences should be articulated, understood, recognized, appreciated, accepted, and valued. It is one thing to say that you want to hear new ideas and new approaches, but another thing to embrace a different way of thinking that challenges your basic assumptions about the world.

Equity means more than treating people fairly and giving them access to advancement. It also means recognizing that many people face additional barriers to accessing opportunity. These barriers might include language, access to financial resources, physical ability, educational background, conscious or unconscious bias around weight, skin color, or other physical attributes, or different styles of communication. Inequities are unjust and avoidable, but they are persistent, because institutions and systems have been created to sustain them. If we understand the deep, root causes of barriers and disparities within our society, we will be better able to confront and remove them. Equity does not mean treating everyone the same; it means treating everyone in a way that gives them an equal opportunity.

Inclusion requires the development of collaborative, supportive environments in which diverse individuals or groups will feel and be welcomed and their participation and contributions will be valued. An inclusive climate embraces differences and offers respect, through words and actions, for all people. It's important to note that while an inclusive group is by definition diverse, a diverse group isn't always inclusive. Increasingly, recognition of unconscious or 'implicit bias' helps organizations to be deliberate about addressing issues of inclusivity.

Anti-racism. As Angela Davis says, "In a racist society, it is not enough to be non-racist, we must be anti-racist." Anti-racism means recognizing that the power imbalances that white people have accrued over hundreds of years are a part of the status quo. Merely not acting in a racist way perpetuates that imbalance: only by actively fighting against racism will a more equitable society be achieved.[1]

Recognizing and addressing issues of diversity, equity, inclusion and racism in your organization.

One important first question is: Do the members of your board and staff look like, have similar experiences to, and represent the populations that your organization serves? If not, can you be certain that you truly understand your clients' experiences, needs, and hopes? How can you be sure that the services that your organization provides are the necessary ones, offered in the best way possible?

On a deeper level, even if your staff and board are starting to reflect the served population, does your nonprofit welcome and incorporate your clients into the decision making and power structure of your organization? If your nonprofit works with cultures that tend to respect silence or are less likely to jump into conversations, have you learned how to hold back and listen so that their thoughts, feelings, and ideas are given space to emerge? If the organization's core values include being open to new ideas and strategies, does the board demonstrate this value by being willing to try things outside the comfort zones of its members?

Your commitment as an organization to the values of DEI and anti-racism must be rooted in actions if you are to achieve transformation and success. Where and how is your organization spending its money? Someone might say, "Show me your checkbook and your appointment calendar, and I'll tell you what your values are." Actions, more than words, reveal our commitment to change.

> *One example is how power is unconsciously assigned in relation to height. Consider how common it is to say "look up to someone" as the positive, and "look down on someone" as the negative. This shows how language and cultural attitudes affect how shorter people are viewed. Women, in general, are shorter than men, and people in many other cultures tend to be shorter on average than Americans. As one comes to understand how deeply ingrained such attitudes are in language, it becomes apparent how much effort it takes to change a way of seeing the world.*

How is your organization measuring the changes that you hope to see? Are you and the other members of the organization willing to be uncomfortable? Are your actions intended to result in change, or primarily to pay lip service to the idea of change? Are you willing to learn and support each other as you grow through this process? Think about what structures you can create in your organization to help people work toward substantive change.

> *One nonprofit we worked with had ambitious goals for diversifying the staff and the board, but didn't have a clear plan. A new board member helped them to be more effective by allocating one hour of each of six consecutive board meetings to incorporating those goals into their meeting structure, decision making, and allocation of resources. This structured commitment led to open conversations about bringing people on to the board in a way that was supportive and allowed new members to have measurable impact. By focusing on the changes they hoped for, members began to see progress. Gradually the conversations*

became deeper and more comfortable and they were able to then create
a more effective plan for addressing their goals.

To build a more diverse board and staff, you will need to make space to listen to, incorporate, and welcome new people and ideas. Think beyond recruitment, and focus on retention. What *keeps* people from diverse backgrounds engaged? Have you laid the groundwork to shift your way of doing things? How can you build belonging?

What's critical here is not just individual behaviors, but how organizations and systems uphold and maintain inequities. For example, one public health approach focuses on changing individual behaviors, like cutting back on fast food or stopping smoking. This fails to acknowledge that fast food chains and tobacco retailers are more prevalent in areas where there are more people of color. A lack of green spaces and parks to exercise or walk in contributes to a greater incidence of diabetes and obesity in those communities. A systemic solution with greater impact would call for urban planning to include more parks, lighted streets, and bike lanes, with lobbying for zoning laws that limit fast food chains in areas where marginalized people live and work.[2]

A few steps you can take

Experts in the DEI field say there are measures that can enhance your chances of success as you address these issues within your organization.

- If you don't know where you are, it is difficult to know where you want to go. Start by conducting an organizational assessment to get a sense of the areas where your organization currently succeeds and what level of success it has achieved. There are a number of assessment tools available online. The Centre for Global Inclusion offers a very practical tool that lets you look at different areas of your organization to give you five different levels that may help you measure the effectiveness of your efforts.[3] The Coalition of Communities of Color has another.[4]
- Once you have more clarity regarding your organization's successes and

challenges, strive to come up with some realistic goals. If you can't see or measure progress, it is difficult to maintain forward momentum. You need to overcome the sense that you are just doing this work to fulfill a grant, rather than to make true progress. Set benchmarks, and assess whether you are meeting them or not.

· Remember that addressing DEI issues is often difficult and quite emotional work. We all need to feel supported and see success if we want to make changes. Recognize that this is all a work in progress with no quick solutions. As we learn more about these issues, we grow and transform ourselves as individuals, even as we change our organizations.

· Pick some "easy win" areas. Many people suggest that, after the assessment with the leadership team and the board, you should pick something that you can accomplish in one month. Then, move to another topic that you can reasonably achieve in one quarter. If you can start to feel some success, it will propel you toward additional changes that may be more challenging.

· While having an expert available to help guide you through this process is certainly a benefit, not everyone has access to that kind of help. Don't let a lack of expert guidance prevent you from starting the journey. This is an evolving field, and new materials and ideas emerge every day. Use the free tools that are available, have conversations with other organizations and their board members, and share experiences, tools, and helpful resources.

Learn not only from what is working, but also from what is not. Two examples:

The board of an Hispanic housing agency worked hard to bring on more Latinx members, and they were successful. The meetings were held in English, without formal translation. A couple of the bilingual members translated when "important" issues were discussed. The new Spanish-speaking members felt irrelevant and disempowered and were about to quit. The group hired professional translators for the board meetings, and then alternated between holding the meetings in Spanish and in English so that everyone could experience how it felt to need translation. Participation by the Spanish-speaking members increased greatly. Meetings took longer, but were much more engaging, with new ideas emerging.

We worked with a board that was dealing with an issue that significantly affected Hispanic and Native American populations. They recruited new members from these two groups in order to have community leaders represented and to encourage a realistic discussion of the issues at hand. But they didn't anticipate how their meetings might need to change in order to fully engage the new members. At the first two meetings, the new members didn't speak at all. The board chair reached out to them and realized that it was customary for them to join a conversation only when specifically asked and when there was clear space to do so. At the next meeting, the board chair made a point of asking the quiet board members for their opinions and gave them space to complete their thoughts. It took a while, but gradually other members tried to be quieter and solicit more feedback from the newer members of the board. The tenor of the meetings completely changed.

As you take this on, both the board and the staff need to work on DEI and anti-racism efforts; otherwise, a disconnect can grow between the two groups. It is important to have good communication as you seek to transform your organization. If you hire a consultant to work with you, it is crucial to find a good fit. Talk to previous clients about their experiences. Ascertain the consultant's capacity and training to handle the emotions that will inevitably arise. Approach the work with humility and the understanding that real change will take time. Be excited about the possibilities that arise when you start hearing new voices and new ways of thinking.

REVIEW QUESTIONS

- Do board members and staff have a shared understanding of what the terms diversity, equity, and inclusion mean?

- Is there a commitment on the part of the organization to work together on making progress in these areas?
- Do you clearly understand what you would like to accomplish?
- Have you established guidelines to help you determine whether the organization is making progress or not?
- Is there a person or a small group that is taking responsibility both for ensuring that your organization is paying attention to these issues, and for assessing its movement forward?
- Is the senior leadership of the board and the staff committed to making progress on DEI issues?
- Have you talked as a group about how it feels to be uncomfortable and how you can support each other as you go through unavoidable situations that cause discomfort?
- Is there someone you trust that you can talk to when you feel confused or unsure or unclear as your organization faces these issues?
- Do you see the effects of expanding your nonprofit's efforts to include diversity and inclusion throughout all of your conversations, or only when the members of the board or staff specifically talk about DEI?
- Have you, as an organization, instituted an ongoing assessment process so that you can see where you are making progress?
- Have you found ways to recognize and celebrate your organization's successes and to chronicle the benefits and richness that this work brings to your organization?

1. These definitions draw from many sources, but predominantly from The Independent Sector. www.Independentsector.org.
2. *From conversations with Carol Cheney, Diversity Equity and Inclusion Manager, Meyer Memorial Trust, Portland, Oregon.*
3. Access the tool at: http://centreforglobalinclusion.org/downloads/ You'll need to register, but you can use their information for free.
4. Access the tool at: https://www.coalitioncommunitiescolor.org.

11

WHO'S RESPONSIBLE, THE BOARD OR THE EXECUTIVE DIRECTOR?

C onfusion sometimes arises between the executive director and the board regarding areas of authority and responsibility. When this relationship is clear and there is good communication, organizations tend to thrive. But this connection can vary greatly depending on the people involved and their previous experiences. If you were part of a small nonprofit that had no staff, you would be comfortable with the notion of board members doing everything. Perhaps you were actively involved in fundraising, programming, and public relations. In larger organizations, your responsibilities would likely have been different. Depending on the size and structure of the organization where you first learned about nonprofit governance, you might have a different interpretation of the executive director's responsibility and authority.

In its simplest form, the board is in charge of setting the direction of the organization, approving the budget, and hiring and empowering the executive director to move the organization in that direction with the staff and using the approved funds. While that sounds pretty straightforward, it often is not. The wide diversity of sizes, shapes, and structures of nonprofit organizations can cloud even this straightforward delineation of authority. The key to success is transparency and frequent, clear communication. Let's do a quick review of some specific areas and who is traditionally responsible for each, keeping in mind that these are guidelines rather than hard and fast rules.

Hire, supervise, support, evaluate, reward, and, when necessary, remove the executive director: *Board's responsibility.*

These are some of the most important responsibilities of any board of directors. Few people would argue with the "hire" part of the equation, though the staff has a role to play as well. Are you giving the support and supervision that is needed? Sometimes, years go by without a proper evaluation of the executive director. "Jamila is doing a great job; let's give her a five percent raise this year. We'll evaluate her next year."

The board is responsible for performing a proper evaluation. If the board doesn't offer it, the executive director should request—and, if necessary, help to organize and structure—an effective evaluation. If there is not a regular process for evaluating your organization's executive director, that's a potential red flag. If the director is resistant to an evaluation, take note. As a new board member, this is an important issue to address.

Hire, structure, supervise, and evaluate staff: *Executive director's responsibility*

The executive director is empowered to create the staff structure to carry out the goals for that specific organization. If the goals are not being accomplished, open communication should reveal the causes. An effective executive director should have the skills and experience to best accomplish the mission with the available resources. This includes determining the level of authority and decision making that each staff person should have.

It is the executive director's responsibility to hire staff, ensure that they receive training, and set salaries within the budget. If necessary, the director may reprimand or fire a member of staff, or delegate these tasks to another senior staff member.

Certain staffing decisions, such as the hiring of a development or finance director, may benefit from board involvement. While the final decision is up to the executive director, having the finance or development committee members meet with and give input on final candidates can be helpful. From the candidates' perspective, meeting the board members with whom they would be working closely gives them a clearer picture of what the job will be like.

It may also be worthwhile to involve some members of the board when an executive director is considering firing a senior-level person. That person may have built direct relationships with particular board members. A lack of communication can create distrust between the executive director and the board, just as openness can build the mutually supportive relationships that are needed to function well. It is better to make sure that people are aligned with the executive director's decision before it's enacted, than to have to do damage control afterwards.

The executive director ensures that staff evaluations are done at least annually. Typically, the director evaluates senior managers, who then do evaluations of their own staff. See chapter 17 on evaluation for more information. If you are fortunate enough to have an experienced HR professional on the board, that person may provide guidance and suggestions on how to engage in a good evaluation process; they would not, however, participate in the actual evaluations.

Set overall direction for the organization: *Board's and staff's responsibility*

One of the fundamental jobs of a board is to ensure that the mission, values, and purpose continue to serve a public good according to the organization's charter and articles of incorporation. The board, the executive director, and the staff need to be in alignment, or the organization will suffer. Any major strategic changes must have both staff and board input to be successful. Once the overall direction is clear, the staff has the responsibility to implement the programs.

Prepare for and lead board meetings: *Board chair's responsibility, with assistance*

The agenda of a board meeting is traditionally prepared by the board chair in partnership with the executive director and other board members. Traditionally, the board chair facilitates the meeting. If the executive director takes charge of setting the agenda and also leads the board meetings, consider this a potential red flag, as it may indicate that the organization has a rubber-stamp board that isn't playing the good oversight and advisory role that it should be.

Pass a yearly budget: *Staff's recommendation, with board's approval*

It is the board's responsibility to pass a balanced budget by the beginning of the budget year. It is the executive director, working with the staff, who has the facts and figures and knows the program costs that form the basics of the budget. If your organization has a clear strategic direction, the staff will create a draft budget that is designed to advance it. See chapter 14 for details on budgeting.

Approve contracts and grants: *Board's responsibility*

Who should sign off on a three-year, $100,000 grant to expand your development department or embark on a new program? A grant is a contract—your organization is accepting money to perform certain services, and if you don't perform them, you are liable for the results—even to the point that the foundation issuing the grant could ask for the money back. Most organizations have a set dollar amount above which all contracts must be approved by the board. Many grants require the signature of the board chair as well. Board members should be informed about all grants that the organization is applying for. The board members may well have connections to the foundation, and they should know what they are committing the organization to should the grant be awarded.

Major changes in your organization's programs or strategic direction: *Staff's recommendation, with board's approval*

If the organization needs to downsize staff, cancel or significantly change a program, or launch a whole new effort, there are almost always budgetary considerations. Decisions may arise that affect the direction and viability of the organization. The staff and board should be involved in these decisions, understanding that the director and staff are the people who truly understand the capacity of the organization. As always, the golden rule is good communication. Executive directors shouldn't suddenly spring this on you at a board meeting. A proposal to eliminate a substantial program requires alerting board members ahead of time, or the idea will be met with surprise and emotional reactions. You won't get the kind of thoughtful reasoning that the organization needs.

> *Let's say you would like your museum to build an additional space to house exclusively Latinx art. No matter how closely this aligns with your organization's mission, only by talking with the staff will you have any idea if it is possible. If you decide together that it's possible and worthwhile, then the board approves it, but the staff is in charge of how it gets done.*

Authorize expenditures: *Executive director's responsibility (up to a limit)*

In addition to spending that has been authorized by the budget, it is common for the executive director to have authority to sign checks up to a certain amount without the board's involvement, especially for budgeted items. Large **non-budgeted items** and checks over a threshold (e.g., $20,000) might require a second signature.

Take legal action: *Board's approval*

Any legal action, either on the receiving end of a complaint, or that the organization is initiating, should be done in consultation with and approval of the board. This doesn't mean that the executive director needs to consult the board every time she talks to an attorney.

Signer on the bank accounts: *Executive director and board chair*

One or two board members, usually including the chair and possibly the secretary, should be a signer on the organization's bank accounts, meaning that they have the ability to write checks, make bank transfers, and access all banking information. The executive director and often another high-level staff position are usually signers as well. The board treasurer should have permission to view the accounts. Having effective internal controls will ensure that more than one person reviews the bank statements. It is important for both a board member and the executive director to have some relationship with the bank in case something should happen to either of them.

Prepare audits: *Staff's responsibility, with board's review and approval*

If you need an audit, either the staff or the board may select an auditor, or recommend that an auditor be changed, but the decision should always be approved by the board. While having the same auditor every year is convenient, having a new set of eyes (a new auditor) after a number of years is often desirable. The most important thing is not to fall into a pattern that allows errors to creep in.

Write off accounts receivable: *Board's approval*

At times, organizations may realize that money they are owed is not going to be forthcoming and they need to write off accounts receivable. This can sometimes happen with large or multi-year pledges. Writing off a large pledge can significantly impact the financial status of your nonprofit. The board should always be consulted before taking this step, and it is good to have a policy that specifies when delinquent pledges ought to be reviewed.

One board had a false sense of security concerning their nonprofit's financial stability because they were waiting on a pledge that was two years old. They were sure it would be coming in. When they finally contacted the donor, it turned out that she had declared bankruptcy the year before, and the donation would not be forthcoming.

Review insurance policies and brokers: *Staff updates the board*

Some groups have a wonderfully attentive insurance broker who always updates policies and checks to see what other options exist. But even the most attentive broker won't be aware of changes in the status of your organization, large increases in budget, new program areas, purchases of new property, or major staffing changes. The board should make sure that these policies are reviewed yearly and the board is kept apprised of any updates.

Oversee personnel policies and procedures: *Board's approval*

Your organization should have a policies and procedures manual. If you don't, then one should be created. Keep in mind that manuals go out of date, so they should be reviewed annually to see if they need updating. Recent IRS changes related to conflict of interest or harassment policies increase the importance of doing this. Commitments to DEI should be reflected here as well. It is the board's responsibility to make sure policies are updated.

If your organization is planning to write its first policies and procedures manual, or if it is doing a major revision, the board may appoint a committee to help undertake this job.

Lobby the government: *Staff informs the board or enlists the board's support*

The executive director should consult with the board before having the organization engage in lobbying or advocacy activities. 501(c)3 nonprofits are allowed to talk to government representatives about their interests, but they are prohibited from advocating for specific candidates. They may lobby for certain legislation, but there are some limitations that you should confirm with your state department of justice. Getting political support for your nonprofit's cause or mission can be crucial, and board members are often the most effective lobbyists. It is important to make sure that you and your fellow board members are following the regulations.

Prepare for crisis and external communications: *Executive director's responsibility*

The organization should develop a crisis communications plan that includes outlining who the appropriate spokesperson is. It might be the executive director, the board chair, or a communications person, but plan this in advance rather than wait until you are forced into a last-minute response. If you know where to direct inquiries, you'll be better able to handle major issues that arise. In general, sensitive information should be channeled through the executive director, unless of course the executive director is involved in the crisis.

Report to the board : *Executive director's responsibility*

There is a lot of flexibility in how often reports need to occur and how comprehensive they should be. Board packets distributed before meetings often include an overview from the executive director, sometimes an overview from the board chair, and relevant committee reports. The board should specify what information they would like to see. Sending out reports ahead of time gives members the chance to think about questions and concerns in advance. Board meetings should be used to ask questions, not to read the reports. Reading reports during a meeting depresses everyone and makes them want to go home and never go to another board meeting.

REVIEW QUESTIONS

- Is there written documentation that clarifies the areas of responsibility of the board and the executive director?

- Are those documents reviewed on an annual basis?
- Does the board regularly monitor the overall direction of the organization?
- Do board members clearly understand the differences between the board's role and that of the executive director?
- Does the board have an annual review process for the executive director?

12

LOVING YOUR FINANCIALS

I f you followed this book, you already looked at a lot of financial information as you were deciding whether or not to join the board. Having a clear understanding of the financial position of your organization is one of the most important parts of your job as a board member.

A lot of people are scared of numbers. They think they'll never understand them, or they feel like the numbers are someone else's responsibility. Don't hesitate to ask for help when you don't understand. We guarantee that others will be wondering the same thing, but are shy about asking. This chapter will take you deeper into developing a clear picture of your organization's financial picture.

> *We worked with one organization where the financial statements were prepared by the office manager using Excel. Unfortunately, the statements didn't tie together. Assets didn't equal the liabilities plus equity. The net income on the balance sheet didn't match the net income on the profit and loss statement. Despite getting these statements for years, no one questioned them. No one realized that their financial statements were inaccurate until we pointed it out.*

The good news is that there is a big difference between knowing how to create the financial documents for your organization, and being able to read and comprehend them. As a board member, you only have to understand them and ask good questions. The right question at the right time can save an organization. And sometimes that question is simply: "What does that number mean?" Or, "shouldn't those numbers be the same?"

We have a list of questions for you to consider later in this chapter, but at the most basic level, you are trying to figure out something very simple: Will the organization have enough cash each month to fund its activities? Are you saving some money each year so that you have a reserve fund for emergencies or unexpected opportunities? And is the financial information that you're getting painting an accurate picture of the organization?

The financial statements help you see how much money your organization has, how much money you owe, and how much money you've been taking in and spending in the past.

Having correct numbers is critical. If the financials are inaccurate, no amount of scrutiny of the financial statements will help you. You need to be sure that someone at the organization is tracking the finances in a way that accurately reflects the income and expenses of the organization. If you are uncertain, ask a financial professional to take a look.

You should examine and understand four basic documents: P&L (profit & loss), cash flow projection, balance sheet, and 990.

Each of these documents, especially in larger organizations, can get complicated, but a basic understanding of them puts you well on your way to fulfilling your role of comprehending and overseeing your nonprofit's financial condition. It will be easier to follow these documents if you have them in front of you, so you should ask someone in your nonprofit to provide you with copies. Let's look at each document in turn.

Profit and Loss Statement (P&L)

This is also called a statement of activities or an income statement, and it is normally provided whenever the board looks at finances, which is usually whenever you meet, or at least once a quarter. This statement shows a list of income and expenses for a set period of time (usually a month, a quarter, or a year). Most P&L statements will show both the latest month as well as year-to-date (YTD) figures and compare them to last year's figures. At the bottom of the statement is the net income, which shows whether you made money or lost money that month/year. Some P&L statements will include a breakdown by program so that it's possible to see how each program contributes to the net income. This breakdown by program is called activity-based cost accounting.

To be most useful, the profit and loss statement should be looked at in comparison to the preceding year. This comparison will show if there are any big changes between the two time periods on your balance sheet. An organization that gets most of its income from an end-of-year donor campaign might look like it is losing a lot of money earlier in the year. As long as the organization has sufficient money in the bank, you can see that in previous years you have always had a successful year-end campaign, and there are no big changes, your nonprofit is probably OK.

We were working with an organization that had always done a big fall fundraiser. Their income from this event had been going down for a few years, and so they decided to hold a different event and do it in the spring. In June, when we came to a board meeting, the treasurer was exclaiming how good the books looked compared to last year. That was true, but when we reminded them that they weren't going to be doing their fall fundraiser, they realized that they weren't as solvent as they thought, but they weren't sure how best to track things. That's where the cash flow statement is helpful.

Cash Flow Projection

A cash flow projection will show you month by month how much money you anticipate having at the beginning of each month, how much is estimated to come in, how much will go out during that month, and what the balance will be at the end of the month. If you prepare this for the year ahead as best you can based on expected income and expenses, you will be able to see if you are increasing or decreasing your cash balance and if you will have enough money to get through the year. A cash flow statement will show actual cash to date.

If there are months where cash flow will be negative, where more money is going out than coming in, then you can quickly see if you have enough in the bank to cover that. If not, you may need to get a loan or line of credit to cover expenses during that month. It's better to plan for this in advance, than to scramble for a loan two days before payroll.

Balance Sheet

This document, also called the statement of financial position, is a snapshot in time summarizing all of the things of value that your organization has (called your *assets)*, and all of the things that you owe (called your *liabilities)*. **Assets** include your bank accounts, endowment investment values, your nonprofit's property minus depreciation, and any uncollected pledges or service fees (called *receivables)*. **Liabilities** might include loans that your organization has taken out, bills you have to pay (called *payables)*, credit card payments that are due, or payroll expenses (like unused vacation pay, for example) that you owe, but have not yet paid. We call those *accrued expenses*. Liabilities might also show money for services that your organization must provide in the future for cash that you've already received (*deferred revenue)*.

- **Net assets (equity)** are amounts that are unrestricted (available for your organization to spend), and restricted dollars like endowments or grants for specific projects that can only be spent on certain things or up to certain amounts. Your balance sheet may show accumulated funds (*retained earnings)*: essentially, profits from previous years. If these are negative, your organization has been deficit spending and very likely has more liabilities than assets.
- **Assets** (everything your organization owns or is owed) = **Liabilities** (everything you owe) + **Net Assets** (the difference between all of your assets and your liabilities)

Reviewing balance sheets that show two periods is recommended so that you can compare changes in assets and liabilities. If there are big changes, you need to understand why that is happening.

Remember, the activity between two periods on a balance sheet is represented by your profit and loss statement.

The 990 Tax Return

You can file four types of 990 forms with the IRS, depending on the size of your budget and the kind of organization. For private foundations, you will file a 990-PF if the annual budget is over $25,000. For all other types of nonprofits, if the budget is normally less than $50,000, you can file a **990-N,** known as an electronic postcard. This "postcard" lists only a few pertinent facts about the organization, such as address, contact info, tax ID number, and the fact that your budget is under $50,000.

If your organization's budget is between $50,000 and $200,000, you can file a **990-EZ,** which is usually four-pages long. Many people can do this fairly simple return without professional assistance if they have been accurately tracking their income and expenses. Above $200,000, most others will file the regular **Form 990.** This has grown in complexity over the years, and many organizations choose to get professional help filling it out.

All board members should review your organization's 990 before it is filed to make sure it looks accurate and that it closely approximates the financial statements you have seen at monthly board meetings. Keep in mind that the numbers reported on your 990 could vary somewhat from the annual financial statement because of how the IRS requires income to be classified and reported. They should, however, be "in the ballpark."

To review your 990:

- Look over the income and expense section of the first page. Does it appear to accurately summarize the financials from the previous year?
- Look at the declarations (a series of yes/no checkboxes). Do these seem

accurate?

- Review the notes at the end of the 990. Do these disclosures seem accurate and complete?
- Is the organization meeting its public support requirements? Most nonprofits are supposed to get support from a wide range of people; 501(C)3 organizations are generally required to list donors who contribute more than $5,000.

Some parts of the 990 are confusing in a way that only a document from the IRS can be. Ask the executive director or the financial officers to help explain any parts that you don't understand.

You owe it to yourself and to the organization to be clear about the financial situation of the organization and how it changes over time. Sit down with someone who can talk you through the details of your organization's finances. Ask questions, and get explanations for each line item. Figure out how the balance sheet is tied to the income (profit and loss) statement and the cash flow statement. Each statement tells a story, and your job is to understand the story so that you can anticipate future problems.

One of my most fraught times working with a board involved use of restricted funds. This organization had received a two-year grant totaling $100,000, with $50,000 to be spent each year. I looked at their financials right before the end of the first year. The board was proud that they had managed a $20,000 surplus for the year. They had recorded the $100,000 this year as they were supposed to do. The IRS says you need to book the whole amount the year you get it. Unfortunately, they had not set aside, or restricted, the $50,000 they were supposed to use next year. Instead of a surplus, they actually had a $30,000 deficit for the year. It was going to be a struggle for them to balance their budget the next year.

You should ask these questions to better understand and deal with financial issues.

- Is your organization headed toward having more income than expenses (being in the black), or spending more than it is bringing in(in the red)?
- If you're anticipating being in the red, what is your plan for this?
- Is there a month-to-month cash flow statement, and are there any potential problem times coming up this year when your organization won't have enough money, even if you are projecting a positive cash flow for the year's end?
- If so, what is your plan for this? Will you slow down paying bills, take out a loan, or secure a line of credit?
- If there is not a cash flow statement, how do you know if your nonprofit will have a potential problem sometime this year?
- Do you have a plan to review your organization's budget half-way through the year and re-forecast income and expenses if necessary? Perhaps a big grant you were expecting didn't come in; perhaps your nonprofit received a large unexpected bequest; maybe a pandemic canceled your annual fundraiser.
- Are financial documents sent out at least a week before the board meeting? There could be good reasons why financial statements are unavailable or late once in a while; but if this happens repeatedly, it's almost always a red flag. Be persistent until you understand your organization's financial situation.
- Do you have good internal controls over finances? *Internal controls* means your organization has clear procedures for who can sign checks, who receives and reviews the bank statements, how the organization handles petty cash, and who reconciles the bank statements.
- Does your organization have a line of credit? How much is it, who has authority to draw from it, and what is the process for doing that? The board should be notified whenever the line of credit is being accessed.
- If your organization has a line of credit, do you use it only when you have a realistic plan for how it will be repaid, and are you making sure that plan

is followed? If you join an organization that has a line of credit without a plan in place to repay it, be persistent in asking questions until you are confident that there is a realistic way to repay it, or consider postponing joining the board.

- Do you know who does the bookkeeping for your organization and who does your payroll?
- If you use a payroll service, you can be pretty well assured that your payroll taxes are being paid—but you should ask anyway, in order to be 100-percent certain. This is one of the areas where the IRS can actually come after individual board members for payment of unpaid taxes, so you want to be sure.
- Does the balance sheet include a large "accounts receivable" amount (money owed to the organization for donor pledges or services provided), and, if so, is it realistic or out of date?

We recently worked with an organization that had over a million dollars in accounts receivable on their books. We discovered that these were pledges from a fundraising campaign that had taken place several years ago. With a couple of phone calls, we saw that most of these pledges were not going to happen. People had died or no longer were supporting the organization. The organization's financial situation was vastly different than they had assumed once accounts receivable was adjusted.

Do you need to do an audit or a financial review?

Audit. An audit involves a detailed review of your financials by an outside professional. Auditors will examine your organization's financial statements, bank accounts, board resolutions, and internal control policies. They will often interview key employees and look for red flags that might indicate fraudulent activity. If your nonprofit is receiving federal funds, you will most likely be required to have an audit. Audits can easily cost $10,000 or $20,000, even for smaller organizations. An audit does not guarantee that there is no fraud, but it does give you a better chance of uncovering fraud if it exists.

A Financial Review. A review is a less rigorous version of an audit. It is less expensive and usually relies more on staff to prepare the financial statements. The fact that an organization does an audit or a review can help lessen the chance of fraud simply because a dishonest employee, knowing that the organization is vigilant about overseeing its finances, might be less willing to take the risk of detection.

REVIEW QUESTIONS:

- Do you have access to all of the above documents and have you reviewed them?
- When the financials are presented at a board meeting, do you understand what people are saying, and do you feel confident that you have a pretty accurate picture of the financial health of your organization?
- Do you feel comfortable asking questions about financial matters at the board meeting if you don't understand something? Please ask something! If no one ever asks any financial questions, that in itself is a red flag, because there are almost always questions that ought to be asked.
- Did the board review and understand the 990 before it was filed?
- Are your organization's 990 filings up to date?
- Are there any funds that are restricted? In other words, are there any grants that must be used for a specific purpose, and what is the timeframe for their use? How are they accounted for, and is it clear when and how they are to be used?
- If the auditor has presented "findings," which are things that need to be addressed or corrected, is there a clear plan to correct them?
- Are the financial documents that are presented to the board up to date? For most things, this means no more than two-months old.
- Do your financials include a breakdown by program? Are all programs revenue neutral or positive? If not, do you understand why your organization is supporting a revenue negative (money-losing) program?

13

BUDGETING

The budget is one of a board member's most important planning and evaluation tools. Past budgets let you know how realistic your organization's aspirations and plans were, give you clues about whether you have the community support that you think you have, and help you analyze whether you are using your resources efficiently and appropriately.

Done well, a yearly budget highlights priorities for the coming year, allocates resources, and reaffirms a common understanding among the board, the executive director, and the staff about strategic direction for the coming year. It can reveal areas of potential weakness and looming shortfalls, giving you a roadmap to follow, so you'll know if the organization is on track or in potential trouble as you move through the year. Done poorly—not creating a budget or just copying the one from last year—it becomes a wasted tool, or a document that misleads you and the staff about what you are supposed to be doing.

One group we worked with put extra energy into examining their budget one year, and discovered that they had been siphoning funds from several other programs to fund one that they all had thought was a money-maker. The irony was that the program was not particularly well aligned to their mission, but they were doing it because they all thought it supported their bottom line. They voted to close down the program.

What are the elements of a good budget process, and what is the role of the board? If your organization is on a calendar year, the budgeting process usually starts in the late summer or early fall. Depending on the size of your organization, it might involve the staff, senior leadership, the CFO, or just the executive director who takes the first steps by preparing department budgets. Any anticipated changes, such as a big grant, the closing out of a program, a large restricted donation, funding cutbacks, or a recent strategic plan that determines new initiatives, would all be taken into consideration here. This is a good time to review salaries, because they need to fit into the budget. Are they comparable to similar jobs in the community, and are they fair? Too often in nonprofits, we see hard-working people doing stressful jobs, but not being compensated fairly, or having to work without needed equipment. Are members of staff at your organization being asked to do their work on obsolete or shared computers that limit their effectiveness?

Once staff has created an initial draft, the finance committee goes over the proposed budget and brings in the development department to be more realistic about what is possible. Check to see that the budget reflects the strategic plan. Are there environmental factors on the horizon that could have a significant impact on the organization? Will the government be cutting back on its funding of specific programs? Are the anticipated revenues for the coming year realistic in the eyes of the development department?

Income from fee-for-service activities may be easy to estimate if it remains stable over the years. You may also have fairly predictable annual donor activity that has a clear trajectory. If you know your organization's funders, and your grant funding has been stable for a number of years, you may be able to project income with some clarity.

Once the draft budget has been vetted by senior staff, the finance committee, and the board chair, then the entire board will need to review it. Most people need preparation to understand a budget. The proposed budget, along with notes and explanations of any changes from the previous year, should be received by the entire board at least a week before the meeting in which you are going to vote on it. The executive director and the board chair should try to anticipate possible questions and encourage board members to study the budget and ask about anything they don't understand. Ask them to send any substantial concerns to the finance committee ahead of time in case additional research needs to be done.

Allow enough time on the agenda for a thorough discussion and clarification. Expect that it will take longer than you think to explain some items. Be excited when board members ask tough questions. Keep in mind that the board's approval is about the feasibility and the strategic direction of the budget. Don't question fifty-dollar line items—leave that to the staff. Look for big trends and discrepancies.

Ideally, you will vote to approve a budget by the end of the year. Sometimes, the final approval bleeds over into the next month, after the new fiscal year starts. A little bit of slippage is not a big problem, but you shouldn't be passing the budget several months into the new year.

Adjust the schedule accordingly if you're on a fiscal, rather than calendar, year. A fiscal year is a year that, for budgeting and accounting purposes, begins some time other than January 1st.

Cost accounting

One strategy that helps organizations understand their budget allocations for specific programs is to create a *cost accounting* budget. This looks at revenues and expenses by program area and allocates overhead, such as administration, salaries, facilities, and insurance, to each program according to use. A cost accounting budget gives an extra measure of transparency to the real cost of events and programs so that you can make better decisions about how to cross-subsidize programs and activities that are truly focused on the mission.

One nonprofit had a gift store that seemed profitable until the cost accounting budget showed that the salaries for running the gift store were being covered by a different program. When the salaries were correctly allocated, it showed that the gift store was losing money each year, which meant donations were actually being used to support the gift store operations. This didn't make sense in the context of the mission and the gift store was closed.

Another organization ran a yearly art show that was supposed to be a fundraiser. When the full cost of salaries was taken into account, the art show lost money each year. In this case, the board voted to keep the art show, but consider it a program that deserved sponsorship and donation support, because the show supported the mission of the organization. They also stopped identifying the show as a "fundraiser."

REVIEW QUESTIONS

- Have you studied this year's budget and do you understand it?
- Is there a mid-year review and, if necessary, an adjustment built into the plans?
- Do you understand the budgeting process and the role of the board?
- Are there any factors that might result in a radical change in any part of the budget?
- If you were asked to present the current budget and explain it, would you be able to?
- Does your organization have, or would it benefit from, a cost-accounting budget?
- Does the budget reflect the right programmatic focus to accomplish your nonprofit's mission?

14

FUNDRAISING

There is no simple solution to achieve stable funding for your nonprofit. As a board member, you should understand exactly how your nonprofit raises the funds that it needs each year to accomplish its mission. When most people think of "fundraising," their thoughts turn to asking people for money. While that is usually a part of the equation, there are many different methods to secure funding for an organization.

The overall budget is often thought of as a three-legged stool: fee for service, grants or contracts, and donations. Some organizations receive 95 percent of their funding from the government, and while it might be risky to have nearly all of the funding come from one source, it is often quite stable. Others have a large benefactor who provides a yearly donation to cover most expenses. Some nonprofits have a fee-for-service structure that provides a majority of their income. As a general rule, a balanced income stream provides the desired kind of stability and enables your nonprofit to weather a significant loss in one of those categories.

Does your nonprofit's stool stand upright, or does it list strongly to one side? Find out how your nonprofit supports itself by looking at what percentage of the organization's funding comes from some or all of the following sources:

- grants
- corporate donations and sponsorships

- earned income/fee for service
- government funding or contracts
- bequests
- events
- endowment
- reserves
- in-kind donations
- individual donors

> *For some organizations, the COVID-19 pandemic of 2020 hit multiple income streams at once. Organizations that relied on gatherings of people for significant portions of their income (such as at classes, performances, galas, event rentals, museums, and speaker series) saw the elimination of earned income, rental income, and gala fundraisers all at the same time. The drop in the economy also affected corporate donations, sponsorships, and endowment income. For these organizations, it was individual donors, government grants/loans, and reserves that kept their organizations afloat. The bottom line: Having a mix of income sources can provide a measure of resilience.*

Whatever the funding mix, it is your responsibility to understand and assist in these fundraising efforts to ensure the organization's ongoing financial strength.

If the overall funding strategy is well planned, has a multi-year track record, and is not overly reliant on any one stream, you're probably in good shape, barring sudden changes. Let's look at the various methods.

Grants

Grants form a necessary and important part of many organizations' funding streams. It is important to be clear that grants are not bundles of cash waiting to be plucked from a magic tree. Researching foundations, crafting the grants, evaluating the results of your organization's project, and writing final reports all take a lot of time. The cash amount that your nonprofit gets is often less than the amount you request, and the dollars might come with strings attached that could cost more time and money than you had anticipated. Many foundations prefer to support programming, especially new ideas, rather than the overhead that supports all of your nonprofit's work. Accepting a grant could result in starting a new program that costs more than you were awarded.

According to Candid, around 18 percent of all nonprofit support in the United States, or about $75 billion dollars, came from foundation philanthropy in the form of grants in 2018, a record year. Despite some challenges, this most likely will and should form a part of your organization's yearly support.

There are many books about how to research and write good grant proposals. If it makes sense for your organization to raise funds with grants, it's worth spending time learning how to put an effective grant strategy in place. Research and relationships are key. Applying for a grant for something a foundation has never funded before wastes time and energy. Talking to a program officer who can help you understand the goals of the foundation can save time and focus your efforts. Building a relationship with a program officer who comes to believe that your program is valuable and that your nonprofit has the experience and expertise to make good use of the funds is even more important.

Corporate donations or sponsorships

Corporations donate over $40 billion a year to nonprofits. Your organization might be able to share in that largess, but you need to understand why corporations donate. The money may come from either the marketing department or the corporate foundation, but it will almost always be linked to making the company look good or improve sales. Some companies only give to a nonprofit if one of their employees is on that nonprofit's board, and many corporations encourage employees to become involved with community nonprofits. So do your research, see where the corporation has donated in the past, understand that an employee presence on your board may be necessary, and try to look objectively at whether your organization makes sense as a place for that corporation to invest.

Earned income/ fee for service

Many nonprofits gain significant revenue from the work that they do. If your organization teaches trauma-informed yoga in prisons, you might charge a fee for training teachers. A photography gallery might sell photographs as well as support artists. A health clinic might receive some payment, even though their services are generally free. Your nonprofit might have a shop that sells used clothing and household goods to support other services that your organization provides, employing some of your clients as an extra benefit. Funds in this fee-for-service category are often relatively stable. Make sure that you take into account all of the expenses, especially salaries of those providing the services, when evaluating whether such activities are actually profitable. If your earned income program is losing money, yet is tied closely to your organization mission, you may decide to continue it, but recognize that it isn't a fundraiser; it's a program that has to be partially subsidized by grants, donations, and other sources of income.

Government funding or contracts

A significant source of revenue for many nonprofits is federal contracts, as nonprofits increasingly take on delivering services that were previously provided by the government. Be aware that many contracts underfund the overhead needed to administer these programs effectively. Understand the true costs, and be prepared to raise additional money from other sources to cover those costs.

The application and the reporting for state and especially federal funding can be more complicated than foundation funding. Federal funding generally requires an audit, which can be disproportionately expensive for small organizations. Also, keep in mind that federal funding priorities may shift depending upon who is in political office, even if your nonprofit is doing excellent work.

Bequests

Significant gifts can come when someone leaves a part of their estate to your organization. In most cases, such a bequest comes as a result of years of cultivation and relationship-building, sometimes over the course of many changes in board members and executive directors. An established nonprofit that maintains long-term relationships with donors has a better chance for a bequest than a freshly minted organization.

Don't forget the people who have pledged a bequest. People give bequests because they believe in the cause and the people who are doing that work, but they need to feel connected.

> One organization had been successful in soliciting a $100,000 bequest, but never did any follow-up to maintain the relationship. Over the years, the donor shifted her priorities, felt disconnected from and unappreciated by the organization, and directed her funding elsewhere. The organization didn't even know they had lost the funding until they contacted the donor many years later and discovered that the money had been redirected.

Events

Events can be significant and predictable sources of income when managed effectively. But galas may also serve more as cultivation "friend-raisers" than as actual sources of income if they cost more to put on than they earn. Everyone has heard stories about enormously successful raffles, walkathons, golf tournaments, and auctions. It's fun to talk about the $100,000 generated by an auction, but be sure to factor in all expenses, including staff time. It is important to look at the true cost and the goals of these events when deciding whether to continue them.

Many events include an "ask" at some point during the program, when a board member or the executive director asks attendees to give money to the organization as a direct contribution above and beyond what they might normally give. These "asks" are important components to the program and should be choreographed just as carefully as the dinner, the auction, or the other presentations.

> *I was the executive director of an organization that held an annual dinner fundraising event. We showed off the great work that the organization had done all year. The food was amazing, and the feeling in the room was generous. We turned "the ask" over to a celebrity who was a supporter of ours. Unfortunately, she didn't know our programs well enough to make a passionate pitch for support. Her ask was weak. I realized I should have made the pitch myself because I knew how to celebrate our work. I had given this important job to someone else, because I thought a celebrity could do it better.*

Asking for money is like any other skill. If you practice it and get feedback from people who are good at it, you will get better. Most good asks are based on telling your nonprofit's story and then giving someone an opportunity to participate if they are moved by your words. Often, people will make your job easy. They'll ask, "How can I help?" Make sure you're ready to answer that most basic of questions!

Endowment

Some nonprofits are fortunate enough to have an endowment from which they draw a yearly amount. Laws govern the maximum that can be withdrawn, but most organizations take between four and five percent, which enables them to gradually increase the size of the endowment, while accounting for inflation. Make sure that you know who invests for your nonprofit, who is monitoring the portfolio, and what the investment strategies and withdrawal guidelines are.

Reserves (quasi-endowment)

Some nonprofits have reserves that are invested and withdrawn similarly to an endowment, but without the guidelines and restrictions. The advantage is that your organization has more freedom to use this money as it chooses. The disadvantage is that, with freedom, you may be tempted to draw down too much, or be lax about your fundraising efforts, because you can always take money from the reserve while the money lasts.

In-kind gifts

In-kind gifts are donations of products or services instead of money, and board members can get very excited about acquiring such gifts through their network of friends and colleagues. This type of donation can be great, as long as the product or service is needed. It is even better when the donation offsets funds that your nonprofit would have had to spend. But not all in-kind gifts help the organization.

> *A woman donated all of her husband's woodworking tools to a nonprofit on the condition that they couldn't be sold. The organization accepted the donation without considering it carefully. The organization then spent years moving, storing, and fixing the tools, even though they were almost never used for programs. The cost of storage over the years exceeded the value of the tools.*

> *At another organization, a corporation offered to donate a giant wooden sculpture that no longer fit in their boardroom. Accepting the donation would not have helped the nonprofit, and instead would have burdened them with caring for and storing the sculpture indefinitely. The nonprofit declined the gift.*

If you do accept in-kind gifts, make sure that they are useful or salable.

A financial note: In-kind donations show up as income and equivalent offsetting expenses on your profit and loss statement, so they do not increase your net income. In-kind donations of time don't show up at all, but can be considered volunteer hours. Donors may want a tax receipt for an in-kind donation, but in-kind donations of anything other than physical goods are probably not tax deductible.

Individual donors

Most nonprofit organizations are fueled by the generosity of the community, through donations made during active fundraising efforts. In fact, about 68 percent of charitable contributions to nonprofits in 2018 came from individual donations (around $292 billion).[1] New board members often fear that they'll be asked to fundraise or give a lot of money. Before you get too nervous about this task, let's break down what this really means.

It is critical that you have a fundamental belief in the mission and values of your organization. If you love being on the board of your nonprofit, it's rewarding to donate your time and money to the cause. Your friends who have similar values and interests may also appreciate the chance to share in this work. You are giving people the opportunity to make a positive difference in their community. When you share your excitement about the mission, they will often want to help without you ever asking them for a dollar.

When you fundraise for your nonprofit, it is important to be clear about what the mission means to you.

- Why are you involved with this organization, and what inspires you about the mission?
- What personal stories or life experiences with this organization have affected you deeply?
- What are the results or impacts of the programs?
- What would happen if this organization didn't exist?
- What is your "elevator pitch" to describe and promote the organization?

The answers to these questions will introduce your organization to others and invite them to join you in supporting efforts that you care about. Fundraising is often more relational than transactional.

> *I met one of my favorite board members at a small fundraising event. At the time, "Lisa" was just another donor, but I saw how excited she was about the work and the mission. She engaged every member of the group in conversations. I asked if she would be interested in increasing her involvement with the organization. While flattered, she also was unsure. She had never served on a board and knew nothing about fundraising. But she was open to sharing her excitement with others.*
>
> *"I don't know any rich people," she said. Yet she was able to come up with names of several people who might be interested in the organization and had a track record of giving to other nonprofits. It turned out that Lisa was very well connected and had deep relationships in the community. With a little bit of training and support, she became a leading fundraiser.*

Many boards have a suggested minimum giving-level for each board member. Some also have a suggested give/get goal—which means that, as a board member, you are not only expected to give, but also to get funds from others. Before joining a board, make sure that you're aware of all such expectations—and that you're prepared to commit accordingly.

Board members contribute to fundraising success in many ways, beyond just 'making an ask.' Fundraising is a process and includes a broad range of activities. It should be seen as a team sport—not just the work of an executive or development director.

> *The board was trying to decide between two executive director candidates. Both were skilled, but one "had a great rolodex." The board assumed that bringing her in would solve all of their fundraising challenges, and they were thrilled to hire her. Unfortunately, once she started, they quickly learned that a great rolodex does not always equal*

fundraising success. The folks that she was connected to did not have an interest in this new mission she was working on.

The six Rs of fundraising

We sometimes think of fundraising as the six Rs: research, romance, request, recognize, retain, and raise. As a board member, you may have the skills and interest to participate in all of these areas, or just a few. Pick the ones that you enjoy or want to get better at.

Research reveals where your best donor prospects might be and where else you might find people connected to your mission. As a board member, you could be involved in reviewing lists of current donors to see if you know any of the people listed, can share additional information about potential donors, or are able to suggest potential new donors.

Romance refers to how you are going to help people love, or at least get more interested in, the work of the organization. What kinds of things can you do to bring people closer to the work? What stories can you tell to captivate them?

Request is often seen as the hardest part of fundraising. But if you are engaging donors authentically and building their excitement about the work of the organization, the "ask" is a natural culmination of the relationship. It should never come as a surprise to the potential donor.

Recognize the people who support you. An important part of the fundraising cycle is thanking people. Board members can write thank you notes, make phone calls, or just acknowledge the gifts of donors. People feel good when they donate, and they feel even better when someone recognizes their support.

Retain existing donors; it's always easier than acquiring new ones. Put strategies in place to keep donors by sharing the organization's successes and inviting donors to events on a regular basis.

Raise contribution levels. Many people start off donating at a fairly low level. If you continue to build a relationship and give opportunities that fit with their interests, they often give more. Do your homework, and treat people as you would like to be treated.

Easy things you can do on your own:

- Be an ambassador for the organization in your life outside of board meetings.
- Make a significant gift yourself. It is easier to ask others once you have given.
- Ask your employer to match your gifts or sponsor an event.
- Set up speaking engagements at community groups or service clubs where the executive director or key staff can speak about the organization.

REVIEW QUESTIONS

- Do you know how your organization raises the money it needs?
- Do you have a clear understanding of your own role in raising this money?
- Do you know how stable these various sources of funding are?
- Are you willing to learn more about raising money?
- Is there a development plan for the year, and has the board reviewed it to make sure it is viable?
- Is your organization keeping its donors engaged and loyal?

15

STRATEGIC PLANNING

I n his book, *The Advantage,* Patrick Lencioni says, "An organization's strategy is simply its plan for success. It's nothing more than a collection of intentional decisions a company makes to give itself the best chance to thrive and differentiate from competitors." If the board has figured out values, purpose, and mission, then strategy is everything an organization does to accomplish its mission. It is the systems and programs that you execute in order to accomplish the big goal. The strategic plan is a tactical roadmap that the staff develops to steer the organization in the direction set by the board. It should be a joint effort between the board and the staff. The staff has the knowledge and the responsibility to make sure the hiring and compensation systems, program activities, facilities, events, outreach, and everything else that the organization does all support the fulfillment of the mission. Given their responsibility for executing the strategic plan, it makes sense for the members of staff to take a major role in creating it.

A strategic planning process often starts with confirming the organization's values, purpose, mission, and vision—the elements that we talked about in chapter nine. As board members change over time, it is worthwhile to reaffirm what you are doing as a nonprofit and why you are doing it. The board should understand as clearly as the staff the strategies that will be employed to get there.

As a new board member, your first questions are often basic. Is there a strategic plan? Is it up to date? Is it being used by both the board and the staff? Do you understand it? Does it align with the work plan of the executive director? The answers to those questions will tell you a lot about the state of your organization. If there isn't a plan, how does your organization know what direction it is headed in, and how do individuals know their work is supporting that direction?

Some organizations spend tens of thousands of dollars to hire consultants, create elaborate strategic plans, involve and listen to the community, talk to stakeholders, or make big strategic shifts. Some go it alone, with a one day meeting of the staff and board to reaffirm the organization's direction and brainstorm new ideas. Some have nothing at all.

Do you need a printed plan? It all depends. Occasionally, foundations will ask to see your plan as they consider whether to fund you. A written plan can help the board and the staff navigate the landscape they will traverse as they fulfill the mission. You need to anticipate the funding, human resources, and physical assets that will be needed to keep the organization on track for the next several years. Having the strategy in writing helps keep everyone on the same page. Don't buy a fancy cover for your strategic plan. It will look too good just sitting on the shelf. You need to use it!

> One organization's strategic plan consisted of just four pillars of activity that were designed to help fulfill the mission. Each pillar was fully described in the written plan, and it was easy for everyone at the organization to remember the four areas of focus and decide if the work was helping or hurting those four areas. The strategy led them to raise money to fix their buildings, increase earned income to raise staff salaries, and devise a system to hire good people who fit the staff culture. The executive director worked with staff to develop the strategy and then presented it to the board, who approved and supported it by making sure budgets and fundraising were tied back to the strategy.

As a board member, you need to understand how your nonprofit assesses its progress, how it makes strategic decisions, and what guides that decision-making process. Some organizations have a website that publicizes what they do, whom they serve, what their values are, why they deserve support, and how they will solve the problem they are addressing. Not all groups need an official document titled "strategic plan." But they do need to know the elements that are outlined above.

Whatever document your organization has, ask the following questions to know if your plan is useful or not useful:

- Does it help you decide what to do or not do?
- Does it inspire you?
- Does it guide your work as a board?
- Does it provide clarity about where to put your focus and your energy?
- Does it help you evaluate whether the executive director and the organization are going in the right direction?
- Does it drive fundraising goals?
- Is it current, expired, or about to expire?
- Does it help you identify when to celebrate successes?
- DO YOU USE IT?!

If your organization decides to create or update a strategic plan, the process should involve both the staff and the board. Many organizations create a strategic planning committee that meets with the executive director and senior staff to decide how to proceed. They make decisions about whether to bring in outside facilitation help, how broad a scope is needed, how many years the plan will encompass, what roles the staff and board will play, and what the final form of the plan will look like. Once again, the members of staff, with primary responsibility for executing the strategic plan, should also have the primary role in creating it, tracking progress, and keeping it updated. The plan is their roadmap for action, and it should be "owned" by them.

If the mission, vision, values, or purpose of the organization are ambiguous, you'll be setting yourselves up for failure. Many strategic planning processes reaffirm those elements before getting into the strategy part. Ask good questions, keep the mission in mind, and make sure that, at the end, you can explain to someone else how the strategy aligns with the mission.

The difference between a strategic plan and a business plan

A business plan analyzes the impact of a program on the organization and how it will affect staffing, finances, buildings, customers, and marketing. The business plan makes the case *for* or *against* pursuing that new line of business. Business plans contain financial, historical, market, and programmatic analyses. A business plan may be conducted as part of developing a strategy. For example, you might analyze whether adding a new building will help fulfill the mission or swamp you in debt. The results of a business plan can tell you whether a particular action makes sense and should be pursued. A strategic plan may include one or more business plans.

REVIEW QUESTIONS

- Does your organization have a strategic plan? How is the plan being used?
- If your organization is reviewing or creating a strategic plan, is everyone clear about expectations for involvement?
- Can you clearly explain what you hope your nonprofit will accomplish in the world and what your organization's plans are to accomplish that?
- Will your organization's strategies help you accomplish your nonprofit's mission?

16

BOARD RECRUITMENT

This book began with an example of a casual approach to recruiting. Hopefully, by now you understand the need for a thoughtful process that will bring the right people to your board. Board recruitment is often an afterthought, but it needs to be more like long-term financial planning. The right investment today can pay huge dividends in the future. Think back to when you were recruited to the board. Were people clear about what they hoped for and expected from you? Were they forthcoming about everything you needed to know about the organization? Did you receive all of the materials and information you needed? Was there a good process to incorporate you onto the board? Did you feel welcome, useful, and energized? Board recruitment doesn't end with a new person coming to a meeting. That's the beginning. If there's a good process for making new people feel welcome and useful, they will stay and be productive.

Expanding your board

What kind of person do you want representing your organization? What values and experience does a stellar board member have? Humility? Vibrant personality? Program experience? A talent for asking thoughtful questions? A tendency to be a contrarian? Financial expertise? Who is going to help bring out the best in your group?

A competent and energized board supports and attracts an effective executive director who brings in great staff. Recruiting board members is a forward-looking activity that will shape the long term direction of the organization, so think about how the people you pick will affect the organization's success 5, 10, or 15 years from now. The organization needs board members who are committed to helping the organization accomplish its mission, which means a lean board with hard-working members is better than a bulked-up one with the wrong people.

How to find new board members

Finding new board members is not unlike finding donors. You are reaching out to people who have a potential interest in what your organization does in the community. Some people want to give your nonprofit money and be left alone, some people want to volunteer, and some might like to take a leadership role in your organization. The process of getting to know them will reveal the most positive roles for them. Here are some pointers:

- This is not a one-meeting endeavor. Keep in mind the extent to which one personality can change the tenor of a group, and be clear about the skill sets that you are looking for. More interaction between existing and potential board members before new members join leads to a better chance of a successful relationship. Try to have several people "waiting in the wings"—people who have been vetted and are excited about being a part of the board. Set up a timetable so they can join when others roll off. Find ways to keep them engaged, and get to know them better while they're waiting. Remember, they'll still be evaluating their decisions to serve on your board.
- Look for people who are already connected to your organization, either as colleagues of current board members, or more directly, as individuals involved in your nonprofit. Think about donors, program participants, volunteers, and members of a board committee. Multiple interactions between prospective board members and your nonprofit allows everyone

to get to know one another and gives the newcomers a chance to become attached to the mission.

- Involve the executive director and senior staff in identifying and recruiting potential board members. Your organization's leaders are often well connected in the community, know who supports the mission and can talk persuasively about your needs.
- If you're receiving foundation support, you might ask your program officer to share the name of anyone who could be a good fit for the work that you do.
- Talk to community leaders, provide an overview of the organization, and ask them to suggest people that could be introduced to the organization.
- Keep recruitment of new board members at the forefront of everyone's attention. Always be on the lookout for people who might want to be more involved with your organization.
- Think about how you were "found" and recruited to be on the board. Does that process suggest someone who you might approach?
- Many boards have a "board recruitment" committee, whose task is to seek out and vet potential new members.
- Create a matrix that shows the skills that your organization is looking to add to the board, and talk to your contacts about people with those skills who you might want to try to recruit.
- Be open to any opportunities to meet potential new board members.

At one organization where I served as interim director, we made a much needed change to our bookkeeping position. During the transition, we found in a drawer four old donor checks that had never been cashed. I called each of the donors to apologize. All of them said we could keep the donations, but one donor added some thoughtful suggestions for systems we might use to avoid future mishaps. I suggested that our board chair talk to him, and she set up a lunch to talk about possible board service. He joined a year later and brought some helpful perspective on board systems and processes. It all started with a phone call to apologize for a three-year-old mistake.

Often, people think that the secret to success will come from recruiting wealthy donors who can write big checks. These donors may not be the best choice for board membership. They might serve on multiple boards, and their time and energy may be divided. If they are interested in your mission, consider finding other ways for them to contribute. As you get to know one another, you'll have a better idea of whether they would be good additions.

Diversity and Equity

We talked about diversity, equity, and inclusion (DEI) and anti-racism in chapter 12, but let's address this specifically as it relates to enhancing your board. How do you ensure that the people on the board are representative of the community that your nonprofit serves? Is the board truly committed to these issues? Some boards push to diversify because funders demand it or expect it, but efforts motivated solely by a desire to appease funders rarely move your organization in the desired direction.When you add to your board, consider your DEI efforts as a strategy toward better serving your mission, rather than a matter of checking off boxes by making token additions to your board.

Interestingly, according to a recent report by Board Source, board diversity has not increased over the past few years. In fact, many organizations report very few efforts to expand diversity on the board despite the increasing focus.[1]

Be sure that prospective members are aware of how they will be incorporated into the board and become effective participants. You and your fellow board members might want to ask yourselves some of these questions:

- Is it a certain voice and background that is being sought, or is skin color/gender/disability/veteran status being used as a proxy as a result of assumptions about a person's background and voice based on these attributes?
- What track record does your organization have when it comes to providing opportunities for people from varied backgrounds?
- How can your organization truly benefit from increasing diversity? Are

you diversifying for diversity's sake?

- Is your organization self-conscious about your lack of diversity?
- If your organization has clearly defined core values, how well do new board members' personal core values line up? Bringing in new voices where the core values are out of alignment will be challenging.
- Has your organization done a diversity assessment to understand where it has been successful and where it is still challenged?
- Will a new board member be the only person representing your DEI efforts?

Board applicant questions

The kinds of questions that prospective board members are asked when considering board membership can tell a lot about the organization. Are current board members linear thinkers, creative, organized, off the wall, interested in how you think, good listeners, or pontificators? Here are some things you should consider as you are getting to know an organization as a test for your "fit."

- What are you hoping to get out of your board service?
- What are you hoping to give?
- What was your meaningful contribution to another board?
- What about this nonprofit's mission resonates for you?
- What particular benefit (or secret ability or board superpower) would you bring to the organization? For example, you might be good at helping people develop a clear mission, or you might be good at keeping people on track.
- What are your concerns, if any, based on what you've seen already?
- What opportunities do you see, as someone with an outsider's perspective?
- What else do you need to know about this nonprofit before considering board service?

When a board member departs

A lot of time and energy goes into recruiting people to be volunteers, donors, community contacts, mission champions, and board members. All too often, the person you've spent three or six or more years with, who has contributed money and sweat and worry, is sent off with a nice card or certificate and is then forgotten, except for the annual appeal letter.

Your nonprofit needs to stay in touch with former board members and current board members can help with this. Continue to nurture these relationships, and they will pay big rewards. Former board members have a deep understanding of your programs and your organization. They carry the history of the organization and often have great connections in the community. Don't let them slide out of your nonprofit's life. As someone leaves, schedule an exit interview with the executive director and the board chair. People who are about to depart might be willing to share insights that they were not willing to share as an active board member. Find out what kind of relationship they want to have after they leave and how they would like to continue to contribute to the success of the organization.

One board member had a family foundation and gave an annual gift of $20,000 to the organization each fall. She spent time with the executive director to discuss the organization's needs and would then meet with her family to confirm that the gift was being put to the best use to express their family's wishes in philanthropy. Shortly after she left the board, there was a leadership transition in the nonprofit. The new executive director was unaware that this former board member was an annual giver. The former board member was not approached by the new executive director to continue the relationship, and no one on the board thought to protect that relationship. When the new director finally realized that a major donor had stopped giving, a year and a half had passed. It took some time to rebuild that relationship.

REVIEW QUESTIONS

- Has the board clearly articulated the skill sets and interests the organization is looking for in new board members?
- Is there a thoughtful process for attracting new people and vetting them?
- Have there been open conversations with the potential board candidates so that they have a clear idea of what they are committing to do, and what they hope to get out of being on the board?
- Have you done your best as a board to ensure that your efforts to diversify will provide a welcoming and inclusive atmosphere and have a good chance of success?

1. A NATIONAL INDEX OF MUSEUM BOARD PRACTICES Leading with Intent, from Board Source, page 9, and 12-14. https://leadingwithintent.org/wp-content/uploads/2017/09/LWI2017.pdf

17

EVALUATION

E valuation tools help you to understand how effective you are. Used properly, they will help measure successes and identify areas that need improvement. The board is traditionally involved in two areas: evaluating the executive director and self-evaluation as a board. Yearly evaluations are critical. Find out when the last one occurred and when the next one is scheduled.

Executive director evaluation

A well executed evaluation of the executive director is an important tool for ensuring good communication between the board and the director. It presents an opportunity to talk about ways that the board and the executive director can better support each other. The evaluation should not be a time for surprises. If there is a problem on either side during the course of the year, it should be addressed and dealt with as it arises, not at an artificially established time. What you want to avoid is the scenario an outside consultant might confront, in which the board of directors says, "Our executive director really isn't working out. Can you come in and lead us through an evaluation process so we can fire him?"

As interim directors, we've worked with a number of clients who discovered that staff had been poorly treated over a period of years by the previous executive director. In most cases, the board missed many warning signs. Issues of high turnover, lack of communication between staff and board, low-level grumbling in the form of rumors were all ignored by the board. Being respectful of the appropriate boundaries between the board's and executive director's roles in matters pertaining to the staff can sometimes lead board members to steer clear of the staff entirely. As a board, your job is to stay out of the day-to-day business of the executive director, but still create opportunities to listen to the tenor of the staff's observations about the executive director's leadership. This is a delicate skill, because it involves listening with the understanding that there are always multiple sides to a story. A single complaint is par for the course, but a swelling body of complaints can signal that something is wrong. If you have established a clear tradition of communication between the board chair and the executive director, dealing with issues as they arise will be more natural and perceived not as a threat or challenge to authority, but as a normal part of the board's obligation to understand how things are going.

There are many tools and ways of conducting an executive director evaluation. Some involve a couple of board members and the director; others expand that to include members of the staff and community, clients, and the entire board. One effective method involves a self-evaluation that asks the executive director to answer the following questions:

- What went well this past year? What would you like to continue?
- What didn't go as well as you would have hoped? What would you like to change?
- What are you looking forward to this next year?
- What extra things are you doing to promote the values, purpose, and mission of the organization?
- What additional support do you need from the board to be successful?

If the executive director answers these questions as a written narrative, and then the reviewer adds validation and/or contrast to the narrative, you will have a basis for the most important part of the evaluation: an in-depth discussion about how things are going and what the future work looks like.

Another method is a 360-degree evaluation: this involves talking to a wide variety of people who interact with the director in various capacities. These 360-degree evaluations need to be carefully vetted, because often they are simply designed to emphasize the search for problems, rather than the discovery of the many things that are going well. Used correctly, however, they can give a whole picture of how the executive director is performing in multiple parts of her job.

Regardless of the method used for the evaluation, the end result should be a clearer picture of how everything is working as well as any areas needing more support and resources. When finished, the review should provide an accurate sense of the executive director's success at executing her core responsibilities:

- Has the executive director put together the right team? Are there staff retention issues?
- Has the executive director provided a clear picture of the nonprofit's mission, vision, values, and strategy, along with the programs to realize them?
- Has the executive director communicated that mission clearly to the board/staff/community?
- Has the executive director ensured that there are sufficient resources to achieve these goals?
- Are the goals of the organization being met?

And finally, it's important to discover whether the executive director feels supported by the board.

Board evaluation (individual and group)

It can be helpful to do an evaluation of the board's effectiveness as a whole, as well as an evaluation of individual board members. You may run into pushback, like, "I'm a volunteer! Why should I have to be evaluated?" Answering the following questions can help to make sure that your nonprofit is maximizing the health and effectiveness of the board:

- How well is the relationship between the board and the executive director going?
- How do you know it's going well?
- Is the board working together effectively as a group?
- Are there things that could be changed to make the group work better?
- Are meeting times working for everyone?
- Do you have the right number of meetings per year?
- Do the meetings feel productive?
- Are agendas and other information sent out on time?
- Did the board set goals for the year, and have they been accomplished?
- Are expectations for financial support by board members being met?
- Are board members getting personal satisfaction from being on the board?
- What specifically does each board member want to learn about, or contribute to, in the next year?

A simple survey, done anonymously (using technology such as Survey Monkey or a similar online tool), can serve as a basis for good conversations about how things are going. For each board member, a yearly meeting with the board chair and the executive director can help to build a strong relationship that will pay dividends throughout the year—enhancing participation and enthusiasm, identifying areas for improvement, and often increasing donation levels.

Staff and program evaluations

The executive director and senior staff, depending on the size of the organization, are responsible for regular annual staff evaluations. These write-ups go in each staff member's personnel file and are confidential. In most cases, board members don't and shouldn't have access to these files. The board's role is to ensure that good evaluations happen on a regular basis. It bears repeating, because this confusion arises frequently: It is not the board's role to review staff evaluations.

Program evaluation is often done in conjunction with grant reports if the nonprofit receives funding from a foundation. Evaluations should be conducted, regardless of whether you owe them to a foundation. Knowing that your organization is doing effective work is critical to making a case for financial support. The executive director or senior staff members often share these reports with the board to ensure that the goals set out in the strategic plan are being met. As a board member, it's okay to ask to see program evaluation reports. Be conscious, however, of how much extra work you are creating for staff when you ask for reporting information, especially if your request is more about satisfying idle curiosity than answering fundamental questions about the effectiveness of the organization.

REVIEW QUESTIONS

- Is the executive director evaluated on a yearly basis?
- Is there a yearly evaluation of the board?
- Is there a process in place for annual staff evaluations?
- Do you have a clear picture of how effectively the organization is meeting its goals?
- Are there clear evaluation measures for each program outcome that the organization is trying to achieve?

18

EMERGENCY SUCCESSION PLANNING

T he departure of an executive director can be one of the biggest challenges that a nonprofit faces. As a new board member, finding out how prepared your organization is for this transition shows you how involved the board is in its oversight. Is there a plan for your director's departure? Who, besides the director, has access to all of the director's information? Who has the key to the personnel files? Who can access the passwords to all of the online accounts? A good succession plan is essential.

Emergency succession plans are designed to cover the initial phase of a sudden departure of the executive director. Your emergency succession plan should include information about, and access to, the following:

- With the director gone, who will be in charge? Is it a senior staff member, an interim director, the board chair, or someone else?
- Who will be in charge of communications related to the departure? Who will handle communication to foundations and lead donors, and who will be the spokesperson in the event that someone, including the press, calls?
- Who, besides the executive director, has all of the passwords and access to the accounts? Getting into the director's computer is only the first step. The website, the bank account, the database, payroll, accounting software, and social media accounts all have passwords. It's not unusual

for an organization to use 80–100 online services, each of which has a password (hopefully unique).

- Who has access to the bank account and authority to remove the departed director from the account? Is there at least one board member in the role of backup signatory? With no board members signed on to the account, it might take days to gain access.
- Who can make investment decisions, and who knows when CDs come due?
- Who knows about your foundation grants, especially federal grants, including application and reporting deadlines? Is there a master list of pending grant reports? Usually, there are passwords, and it can be embarrassing to ask the foundation how to access your own grant.
- Does some member of the board or staff have access to email and social media accounts? Who has permission to create and close down email accounts? If your nonprofit's Facebook, Twitter, or Instagram accounts are the director's personal accounts, then sorting out who has the rights—the organization, or the departing director who has direct access to hundreds of followers—can be challenging. In a worst-case scenario, you might have to deal with an unhappy departing director who will appear to the account's followers to be speaking in the voice of the organization.
- Many payroll plans are online with passwords. You don't want to miss a payroll because you can't access the account.
- Does a board member have keys to the office, including internal offices, and a key to personnel files?
- Do you know where your backup hard drives are stored, or passwords for cloud storage?
- Is confidential information stored on the server in password protected folders, or is it stored on the director's personal computer? Some nonprofits have allowed the director to use the director's own personal computer for company business in order to save money. This is fine. But electronic documents should never just be stored locally. Using inexpensive cloud storage (Dropbox, Box, Google Drive, OneDrive) ensures that all files are

backed up and can be accessed in case of hard-drive failure, theft, or departure of an executive director.

Make sure that the following are under the board's access or control

- Website access and ability to make changes.
- Cell phone and passwords, if paid for by your organization.
- An organizational chart and work plans for the members of staff, if the organization has these.
- The location of the checks for the checking account.
- The key for a safe deposit box or combination to the safe.
- A board member, usually the chair, should have all of this information written down and stored in a safe place. Be sure to update and pass this along when the board chair changes.

REVIEW QUESTIONS

- Does your nonprofit have an emergency succession plan in place, and does the plan cover most of the elements listed in this chapter?
- Do the officers of the board know where to find the information? A great plan with all the details won't be helpful if only the executive director knows where everything is.
- Is there a yearly review of the succession plan so that it stays current?

19

FINDING A NEW DIRECTOR

O ne of the key responsibilities of a board is the hiring, evaluation, and, if necessary, removal of the executive director.

As we said earlier, the average tenure for an executive director is five to six years and in recent years has been getting shorter. A lot of board members serve for six years, so during your tenure on the board, you may face a change of executive director. What should you know?

The search for a new director is normally at least a four or five-month process, though it may be longer. It is rare to get that much notice about the departure of your current director, so your organization will need to figure out how leadership will be handled between the time that your executive director leaves and a new one comes on board. If your organization has developed a good emergency succession plan, you will be better prepared.

If you have identified a potential successor, you might not need a full search. It is, however, important to be aware of how your choice may be perceived in the community. Is this a logical choice of a qualified person, or an inside deal? If your organization is committed to diversity, equity, and inclusion, will choosing an inside candidate further those goals? Do you have a commitment to offer opportunities to current staff members before searching outside?

Regardless of the timetable, your board needs to form a search committee. Sometimes called a transition committee, it can take charge of intermediate plans for leadership as well as conducting the search. Unless you have a very small board, in which case everyone who is available would be on the search committee, it is common to select five to seven people who will lead the search process. We'll talk later in this chapter about how to consider staff involvement in the search.

Board members are already busy, and adding an executive search to their workload can be a challenge. Many organizations hire an external search consultant—someone who specializes in managing an executive director search—in order to streamline the process, organize the board's efforts, and improve the experience of candidates.

Regardless of whether your organization manages the process on its own, or hires an external search consultant, the following is a typical schedule and work plan for an executive director search process.

Planning (two to four weeks)

Establish a search committee, decide what skill sets you're looking for in a new director, develop a written leadership profile, job announcement, and outreach materials, and start posting the announcement. The skill sets of the departing director may not be the same ones that the committee is now looking for in a new leader. Maybe your organization has grown, shifted some program directions, has a different funding mix, or anticipates a growth spurt. A clear strategic plan that your nonprofit is actively using will facilitate this phase. A key step is to plot the entire process on a calendar, knowing that you might need to be flexible, but enabling the members of the search committee to reserve the important dates. Decide on your organization's salary range for the position, and do research to see if the salary is competitive. Answer the question, "Why is this a good enough position that people will feel motivated to leave their current jobs to come and work here? Too many organizations start their searches without knowing what they are searching for. Spend sufficient time at this stage; involve the staff and sometimes key partners to get clarity.

Outreach (five weeks)

You need sufficient time to attract strong candidates. Merely posting your organization's announcement in a few places rarely brings in the level of candidates that your nonprofit hopes for, nor is it likely to broaden the diversity of your organization. A more comprehensive outreach strategy that actively engages your board, staff, and community supporters is crucial to developing a good pool of candidates. If your organization's goal is to attract diverse candidates, make sure that you and the other representatives of your nonprofit are making one-on-one connections in different communities. Some of the strongest candidates will be people who weren't looking for a new position, but were contacted by someone associated with your organization. If your organization has made it clear from the beginning what kind of person you're looking for, you'll be more effective in your outreach.

Interviews and vetting the candidates (four to five weeks)

Hopefully, you'll be working with your next director for a number of years. Spend the time required to get to know your candidates and make a good selection. If your search committee is well organized and has dates selected in advance, you can schedule interviews and narrow your choices down to final candidates in a few weeks. Make sure that everyone who will be involved in interviewing the candidates is aware of the kinds of questions you can legally ask.

Some candidates are great at interviews, but lack the actual leadership skills that your nonprofit needs. The reverse is also true, so remember that you're hiring for the best director, not necessarily the person who is the greatest at interviews. Reference checking is not a perfunctory task to see if anything bad turns up. It's an opportunity to gain insight into how the candidate performed at previous jobs. Talk to people they reported to as well as people they supervised. If the skill sets needed for this job are clear, it will be easier to ask specific questions about the candidate's capacity in each of those areas. Ask for as many references as you need to complete this picture, and until you are convinced that they have shown in past jobs that they can accomplish what your nonprofit needs.

Remember that an executive director search is a marketing opportunity for your nonprofit. You are out in the community selling the reason that your nonprofit exists and why it is worth supporting. Treat all applicants respectfully by acknowledging their applications, informing them of the timeline, asking thoughtful questions during the interviews, and immediately notifying the applicants who will not be moving forward in the process. A rejected candidate who praises how she was treated is a powerful affirmation of your organizational values.

As more work is done remotely, make sure that everyone involved in the search has the necessary equipment and the training to use it effectively. ZOOM is a great tool for remote interviews, but only if people know how to use it properly. It is critical that they know how to mute, have a good process for asking questions, and recognize that candidates can see their faces at all times. Things you can do in an in-person meeting, like opening a cough drop or sipping coffee, can be distracting and disrespectful when you're on a video screen.

Negotiate an agreement and hire the new director (two to five weeks)

It takes time to negotiate an agreement. Allow the candidate time to give proper notice at a previous job and take a break before starting another all-consuming job as your nonprofit's new executive director.

All of this work adds up to three to five months, so recognize that there will be a period of transition during which your nonprofit's current director will be leaving, or an interim director will be in place. Make sure the members of staff are well informed and looked after.

Onboarding and transition (six to twelve months)

Recognize that hiring the right person is the beginning of the process. Although you will be hiring someone who you believe has the skills and values to run your organization, the board has a responsibility to give the new executive director the best chance for success. Many nonprofits maintain the search committee as a transition committee for the first six or twelve months to oversee this process. Most of what is discussed in this book can be usefully applied to make sure that the new director is performing the way that you hoped. Set up clear, measurable goals and expectations, and then check on the new director's progress after a period of one, three, and six months. Make sure that the transition committee reviews these thoroughly to catch problems and provide support before issues become ingrained. Check in with senior staff members to see how it is going. If this process is set up as an expectation from the beginning, the check-in meetings shouldn't feel threatening to the new director.

Summing up the process

Strong leadership is the key to a thriving organization. If you have an effective search process, your chances of hiring well are good. If you are not sure how to do that, consider getting professional help. Here are a few tips that can give you a better chance for success:

- If you clearly articulate where you are headed as an organization, you are more likely to attract and keep the high-quality leadership that will take you there.
- Being on a search committee requires a serious time commitment. Set up a schedule at the very beginning of the process so that people will know what they are committing to and plan to be available.
- How you treat applicants says a lot about your values and what it would be like to work for your organization. Be organized, responsive, and respectful.
- Involving the staff appropriately gives you a much better chance of success
- Take the time required to know your next potential director. If you need to set up additional meetings to help you make your decision, take the time to do that.

- The best predictor of how a new person will work with you is how they worked with others in the past. Keep checking references until you have a clear picture of how effective the candidate was in the areas that you deem to be most important. Don't hesitate to ask for additional references.
- Put one person in charge of the search process. Choose a person who is totally reliable, has the time to do the job, and will follow through as needed.
- Most qualified applicants may currently be working. This means that the job at your nonprofit must be better, more exciting, more meaningful, and probably better paid than their current work and offer opportunities for growth.
- Hiring the wrong person will cost a lot more in time and money than taking the time to do the search right.

One of the most rewarding searches we've been involved in had two extremely qualified candidates as finalists. Both had all the skills necessary for doing the job and had impressed the staff and the board. We had extended conversations about what we were hoping for, where we wanted to be in five years, and the style and skills we felt were necessary to get us there. As the board, with a clear vision of the future, reflected on our conversations, it became apparent which candidate they would select. That evening, the other candidate called to withdraw her application. She had come to realize that she was not the right fit at this time, and she was so grateful for the in-depth conversations that helped her figure that out. The following month, she became a donor.

Staff involvement in the search process

While selection of the new director is ultimately a board decision, involving the staff in a meaningful way is essential. When the board chooses a new director that the staff doesn't support, it rarely ends well. Recognize that the board will be meeting with the director a few hours a month, but the staff spends much more time. The director will have a huge influence on the culture and atmosphere in the office. With mutual support, your organization can thrive, but without it, you will see high turnover and dissatisfied employees. The quality of service you provide will invariably go down.

Boards often wonder about the advisability of having members of staff on the search committee. It is becoming more common to see staff participate, but with some caution. This is a confidential process, so staff members must understand that they cannot share any information about candidates, even names, with their colleagues. If there are internal candidates, special care must be taken with staff involvement. If you are going to have staff participate on the search committee, here are some recommendations:

- Staff members who are participating on a search committee may need to find extra hours to continue their assigned work in addition to search committee work. They need to be paid for any extra hours or relieved of some obligations during the process.
- Clarify at the outset what kind of communication staff representatives will have with the rest of the staff as you go through the search process. Make sure everyone understands confidentiality issues. Choose one or two staff members who have the trust of the staff and can speak on their behalf.
- A staff member might serve on the committee until the in-person interviews are completed. This staff member might then step off the search committee and participate with the staff instead of the board for the final interviews. Setting separate interviews for staff and board to meet candidates allows for more in-depth discussions. Board members may need to ask for confidential information from candidates that staff members should not hear. Staff may be more comfortable having conversations without the board present and it gives candidates the opportunity to hear staff impressions of the board.
- The staff is often more closely connected to potential diverse candidates than the board. Active inclusion of the staff indicates to a prospective director that empowering your employees is of high value, and this may make you more attractive to those candidates.

- Be clear with the staff and the board members at the outset how staff input will be considered in making the final decision.
- The more confidence that staff members have in the process, the more likely they are to be supportive of the final decision. As long as the rules are clear, it can work well to have members of staff on the committee.

REVIEW QUESTIONS

- Is your organization prepared for the departure of your executive director?
- Is your nonprofit an attractive place to work, with good salaries? Is there a reasonable balance between the executive director's salary and the rest of the staff?
- Is yours the kind of board that someone would want to work with?
- Is there someone in charge of the search who will make sure the process is run smoothly and professionally? Do you need to hire a search consultant to help the board manage the process?
- Have you included the staff in appropriate ways that help them feel empowered in the decision making?

20

CONCLUSION

By the time you've reached this conclusion, you will know enough about your organization and the roles and responsibilities of being a board member to be able to contribute effectively to your nonprofit. If you started this book as you considered becoming a board member, we hope that it helped clarify your expectations, weigh the necessary commitments, assess your passion for the mission, and come to the right decision about whether to join a board. If now is not the right time, you can still contribute financially, volunteer for events or in the office, help with the fundraising, or share your particular area of expertise.

If you have joined the board, it may help to continue to use this book to ensure that your ongoing service is as useful as possible. Keep asking questions to define the ideal role for yourself as a board member. Board composition changes frequently, and the addition or loss of even one person can have a profound effect on the group's dynamics. Maintaining a smoothly functioning board is an ongoing process. Continue to encourage openness, transparency, curiosity, and diversity. It will make your experience more rewarding and strengthen your organization.

Our communities need well-run and high-functioning nonprofits. Now more than ever, we need committed people generating local solutions to the many pressing problems we face. A healthy board sets the framework for good organizational leadership. This is essential for a nonprofit's success, and successful nonprofits help all of us have better lives. There are few things that will bring the same level of joy and satisfaction as being part of a group that is making a profound, positive difference in the lives of others.

Being on a board is a responsibility and a privilege. Board involvement allows you to connect to socially committed people and feel the power that comes with helping our communities. We hope this book provides some of the tools needed to do that well.

May you and your organization flourish!

Acknowledgements

Bob Hazen: This book comes from decades of working in the nonprofit sector, and from the wisdom of the many people I've worked with. Kay Sohl, who co-founded TACS (Technical Assistance for Community Services) leads the list. The depth of her knowledge and the effectiveness of her teaching have illuminated the sector since the 1970s. I'm grateful as well to Guadalupe Guajardo and Cliff Jones, senior consultants at TACS, who taught me more than they might realize. Carol Cheney's insights were essential to the development of the DEI anti-racism chapter. The learning community that we created with the Executive Transition Services (ETS) was a cauldron of exciting ideas and innovation that has made us all better consultants over the past twenty years. Always at my side this whole time has been Paul Lipscomb, a true leader and friend, who has never shied away from a difficult conversation in his life. With Jani, Eric, and Paul, we reignited the energy of ETS by forming Page Two Partners. Each member of this group provides ongoing inspiration and new ideas as we seek ways to support the nonprofit sector. Ben Moorad shared deep insights and peerless editing advice as well. The hundreds of clients we've worked with over the years have filled the pages of this book with the real life experiences that we hope will make it useful for all for readers. And finally, to Joanne Mulcahy, a writing teacher, editor, and wife extraordinaire, who pushed when I hesitated, and comforted when I needed it.

Jani Iverson: It has been an absolute delight to continue to learn and to process our collective experiences through the writing of this book. Working with Bob and Eric, combining years of experience with many different organizations, yielded a rich tapestry to pull from. We all went in to this with the true hope that this information can fast track learning for others — and replicate the successes and avoid the pitfalls we have seen. I'm grateful for all of my colleagues who lead nonprofit organizations and for all of the board members that generously volunteer their time in support of causes they believe in. Working with Bob and Eric has been a reminder of the many fearless leaders that contribute to the nonprofit sector each day.

Eric Vines: Bob Hazen and I first talked about writing this book in the Blue Kangaroo Coffee Shop in Sellwood, Oregon, and since then, it has taken us on a fantastic journey, introducing me to many wonderful people working tirelessly for the betterment of nonprofits. Authors often describe suffering through a collaborative writing process but working with Bob and Jani has been a true joy. I also want to acknowledge Sarah Greene and Marlys Pierson, who served as early role models for how to be an effective board chair. John Gray's Family deserves credit for providing me with essential insights into philanthropy and also helping me see how wealth, channeled with heart, can bring rich and full lives to a wide community. And finally, my wife, my joy, Elsa Stavney, who has been encouraging me to write down my ideas on leadership for a dozen years, and who has provided the space and time for me to work on this book.

About the Authors

Bob Hazen has spent his career working as an entrepreneur, non-profit leader and consultant both in the United States and abroad. Among other adventures, he helped found one of the first curbside recycling programs in the US, started a development office in Vanuatu for the Foundation for the Peoples of the South Pacific, and co-founded a video and television production company focusing on the Soviet Union. In Portland, he built the Executive Transition Services program — a learning community and consulting program that has supported hundreds of organizations in nonprofit leadership and transition. He is currently a partner with Page Two Partners, a nonprofit consulting firm he co-founded with Eric, Jani and Paul Lipscomb. He serves as board chair for Mujeres Aliadas, a women's midwifery and health care project in Michoacán, Mexico, where he lives half of each year.

Jani Iverson has focused on mission-based work for more than 25 years as a volunteer, staff member, executive leader and board member. Her interest in working with passionate, mission-driven people led her to a master's degree in Organizational Development so that she could help corral that passion into informed, structured systems, leading to more impactful organizations. Before coming to Portland in 2005, she served as a Peace Corps volunteer in Western Samoa, where she mentored two national NGO's that supported women and was a founding board member of the country's first HIV/AIDS-specific organization. Since then, as an interim executive director she has helped several organizations through a crisis or transition and has enjoyed the opportunities to nurture and develop multiple teams. She spent nearly five years as the executive director of the Oregon Zoo Foundation, raising funds and garnering community support for the zoo's education, conservation and animal welfare priorities.

Eric Vines has been working in the non-profit sector since 1993, serving as a board member, staff member, organizational leader, and volunteer. Starting as a physics major and then shifting to entrepreneurship and business finance, he loves uncovering an organization's fundamental reason for being. Some of the organizations he has worked for include: the Sitka Center for Art and Ecology, the World Forestry Center, the Gray Family Foundation, and the Franklin Institute Science Museum. He has served on the board of several nonprofits including Business for a Better Portland, the Nonprofit Association of Oregon, the Association of Women Business Centers, and Explore Washington Park. Bringing a strong background in organizational design and culture building, he facilitated cohorts of hundreds of CEOs through the Edward Lowe Foundation's national PeerSpectives™ program which he co-designed and implemented.

14969926R10087